A SPIRIT-FILLED LIFE

Dr. Susan Mbaluka

A SPIRIT-FILLED LIFE

Dr. Susan Mbaluka

Hope Publishers

Houston Texas

Published in the United States by Hope Publishers
Houston Texas

Email: Hopepublisherss@yahoo.com

Layout by Hope Publishers.
All photos credited to Hope Publishers.

Printed in the United States of America

ACKNOWLEDGEMENTS

The support and encouragement of my family were a great blessing in writing this book. My husband, David, Beatrice Lulu, and Wisdom, thank you for walking with me on the journey to serve God through writing. That support gave me peace to focus on producing this book. I love you!

Dr. Zebron Ncube, you went the extra mile in editing the manuscript of this book. Your feedback portrayed the experienced author, pastor, professor, and church administrator you have been for decades. Thank you for taking the time to discuss theological concepts with me. You are a blessing!

Dr. Roderic Bishop, after reading the manuscript of this book, your first response was, "This is an excellent book." That was very encouraging. Thank you. As a church pastor and the prayer coordinator of the Texas Conference, you are one of the busiest people I know. Thank you for taking the time to review the manuscript of this book.

Pastor Paul Muasya, thank you for your valuable feedback on this book. Your leadership and encouragement in ministry is a blessing.

I also acknowledge my prayer partners: Renee, Regina, Kelly, Fay, and the rest of the daily 6:00 a.m. prayer team. You both encouraged and held me accountable to complete this book. I needed it. Thank you, my dear friends. Additionally, I thank the Prayer Ministry team: Elder Gerald Gauthier, Jacklyn, Rose, Mercy, Christian, and all the elders who support our Prayer Ministry and all the members who pray with us every Wednesday evening. Thank you for your perpetual prayers. Even when I am away, you pray for my family and writing ministry. You prayed until this book was completed. May God bless you indeed.

Above all, I thank God for the grace to write and the message to put in this book. God of heaven, You are gracious, merciful, and able. Thank You.

Table of Contents

FOREWORD

It is generally observed that any religion that does not offer power to its adherents is bound to die. Its adherents will go elsewhere to find that power. This is why many people are moving from one religion to another, from one Christian faith to another, and from one church to another. They are trying to find power—spirituality, and zest for life that derives from the Divine. Churches are dying for lack of spiritual power. Pastors and church leaders are trying all kinds of methods, approaches, and programs to revitalize the members spiritually without much success. Dr. Susan Mbaluka seems to have found the cure for the dying spirituality in our churches. In her book, *A Spirit-filled Life*, Dr. Mbaluka is scratching where it's itching. In this book, she has found the itch and the scratch.

I have been honored and privileged to read this book in its manuscript form. My own relationship with the Holy Spirit has been challenged. Dr. Mbaluka argues that as Christians, we are often scared of the Holy Spirit because He will take us where we don't want to go—obedience. Yes, we may desire to be Christians. However, we are often unwilling to go the distance with God. The Holy Spirit is already among us; we are the ones who are not there. I recommend this book to all who desire to see spiritual transformation and revitalization in their lives. Dr. Susan Mbaluka has her finger on the pulse.

Dr. Zebron Ncube, author, church administrator, former professor (Solusi University), and retired pastor (Lake Region Conference).

In my 18 years of pastoral ministry, I have read many books and articles on the Holy Spirit by distinguished scholars, authors, and pastors. However, the power promised by Jesus seems to be absent in churches and ministries to a great degree. Thus, our struggles continue, and we settle for paltry gains when there should be exponential increases. It is evident that the need remains for people who desire eternal life with God to understand and embrace the ministry of the Holy Spirit. This book does an excellent job of discussing this crucial topic.

Dr Susan Mbaluka is a consummate prayer warrior who knows that without the Holy Spirit, we are powerless. She can testify to the power and blessing of the Holy Spirit through her own experiences with the Spirit. In reading the manuscript for this book, it was evident to me that Dr Susan Mbaluka seeks to inform and inspire the reader to embrace the ministry of the Holy Spirit, a message much needed today. Moreover, this book discusses how to receive the Holy Spirit in one's life.

In colloquial terms, using baseball language, Dr. Mbaluka has "hit a home run" with this book. Without fear of contradiction, I recommend this book because I am confident that it will be a great blessing to the reader whether it is used individually or in a group study.

Dr. Roderic Bishop- Pastor and Volunteer Prayer Coordinator-Texas Conference of Seventh-day Adventists

"It is amazing to see how Dr. Susan Mbaluka has surrendered her life to God and allows the Holy Spirit to guide her to serve God through writing. One of the greatest needs for every Christian is the presence of the Holy Spirit in one's life. *A Spirit-Filled life* discusses very crucial matters concerning eternal life. I was deeply blessed by the discussion on the role of the Holy Spirit in our salvation, how we receive the Holy Spirit, and the way the concepts are presented. If you want true transformation and spiritual power in your life. I highly recommend this book for you."

Pr. Paul Muasya- General Field Secretary, AM/SNM/AMR-Coordinator, East-Central Africa Division of Seventh-day Adventist.

INTRODUCTION

The Holy Spirit remains the most misunderstood person of the Godhead. We frequently talk about Him, but we, humans, do not understand how we should relate to Him and how He can be received. God wants His people to be filled with the Spirit (Ephesians 5:18). We read, "Now if anyone does not have the Spirit of Christ, he is not His" (Romans 8:9). What does it really mean to have the Holy Spirit? What does it mean to be filled with the Holy Spirit? Can that be measured as in deciding how much water to pour into a container? Is it like being infused with an electrical current that makes one jump, run around, roll over, and utter an unknown speech? Are miracles the only evidence of the Holy Spirit?

We are told in Romans 8:9 that whoever does not have the Spirit does not have the Savior, Jesus Christ. That being the case, two questions arise for everyone who wants eternal life: Does having the Holy Spirit make any difference between eternal life and eternal death in my life? If it makes a difference, how do I get the Holy Spirit so I cannot miss out on heaven?

The book in your hand, *A Spirit-Filled Life,* discusses these questions and more: who the Holy Spirit is, His role in our Christian and spiritual lives, the best gifts He proffers, and how He makes victory possible in our walk with Jesus. As you read each chapter of this book, you will gain insights into how your walk with Jesus can be revitalized. It is my sincere hope that this book will enlighten you on crucial concepts of eternal life and help you prepare for heaven.

CHAPTER 1

Unseen Danger

There is nothing more dangerous than dealing with a hidden enemy. Often, people identify who their enemies are but may not understand all the ways the enemy will attack. Spiritual warfare is a good example of such. Every true Christian knows that Satan is an enemy. But no human being knows all the possible ways by which Satan will attack or where he may hide to make an ambush.

In this life, we are in a war like the one the Israelites fought against the Amalekites (Exodus 17:8-13). It is amazing that when Moses' arms were raised up, the Israelites prevailed over their enemies. But as soon as the tired arms of Moses dropped, the enemy started winning. Moses did not just raise his hands. He was praying. "Perhaps when Moses dropped his hands because of fatigue, he rested also from the mental concentration necessary to pray."[1] This is another great opportunity to highlight the importance of earnest prayer. Moses' tight grasp on the rod of God and his raised hands showed total trust and dependence on God on behalf of the Israelites.

Understandably, after many hours of raising his arms, Moses became too tired to keep his arms up. And look at God's grace! Aaron and Hur let Moses sit as they held up his arms until the Israelites won the battle. We are at war against Satan and his army of evil angels throughout our Christian lives. We, too, need to keep our minds focused on God. We pray to the Lord and allow the Holy Spirit to dwell in us. We need to depend on God to win the war for us. A strong relationship with God is the only way to victory over Satan and sin. Constant prayer and reading the Word of God keep us in perpetual connection with the Lord. Scripture gives us many promises of power to overcome evil through the empowering of the Holy Spirit.

Think about this, "Christ's humanity was united with divinity; He was fitted for the conflict by the indwelling of the Holy Spirit. And He came to make us partakers of the divine nature."[2] If Christ Himself joined hands with the Holy Spirit to defeat the enemy, who are we not to allow the Spirit to dwell in us and empower us against the enemy, Satan and all his host of evil agents?

The Holy Spirit ensures that we are perpetually connected to the source of the power. Without the Holy Spirit's aid, we will surely suffer defeat against the enemy.

The danger is in relaxing our praying and asking for the filling of the Spirit. A simple distraction from prayer can give the enemy such victory over us.

Satan knows that he can never overpower God's people if they are connected to God. So, he is always watching, preying on the people of God and working to distract them from praying. Even though the enemy attacks all true Christians, he takes advantage whenever he notices a weakness in our connection with God. Even church leaders are not spared the attacks of the enemy, for Satan knows that without leadership, the church loses its sense of direction. Ellen G. White explains this situation very well. She says,

> The power and malice of Satan and his host might justly alarm us, were it not that we may find shelter and deliverance in the superior power of our Redeemer. We carefully secure our houses with bolts and locks to protect our property and our lives from evil men; but we seldom think of the evil angels who are constantly seeking access to us and against whose attacks we have, in our own strength, no method of defense. If permitted, they can distract our minds, disorder and torment our bodies, destroy our possessions and our lives. Their only delight is in misery and destruction.[3]

Unfortunately, while God's people may get distracted and relax from prayer and asking for God's presence in their lives, Satan never relaxes. He is ever ready to take down whoever gives him the chance. Things may look calm, as if we have reached a point where the enemy has left us alone. But no, the evil one is ever devising plans to take us out spiritually.

If only we could have our eyes open to see what Satan and his angels are doing behind the scenes, we would be shocked and terrified. The enmity that God pronounced in Genesis 3:15 is real. God said, "And I will put enmity between you and the woman, And between your seed and her seed; He shall bruise your head, And you shall bruise His heel." Satan hates God's people, and he is constantly working to deceive, mislead to destruction, or even discourage them. Thanks to our loving God, who gave us everything we need for help, including Scripture guidance. In Ephesians we are told:

> Put on the whole armor of God, that you may be able to stand against the wiles of the devil. For we do not wrestle against flesh and blood, but against principalities, against powers, against the rulers of the darkness of this age, against spiritual *hosts* of wickedness in the heavenly *places*...Stand therefore, having girded your waist with truth, having put on the

breastplate of righteousness, and having shod your feet with the preparation of the gospel of peace; above all, taking the shield of faith with which you will be able to quench all the fiery darts of the wicked one. And take the helmet of salvation, and the sword of the Spirit, which is the word of God; praying always with all prayer and supplication in the Spirit, being watchful to this end with all perseverance and supplication for all the saints. (Ephesians 6:10-12, 14-18)

These verses summarize everything we need to do to resist Satan until Jesus comes. As Christians, we must understand that Satan and his army of fallen angels work day and night. They constantly watch and discuss God's people, strategizing how to bring them down. But God gives us ample guidance on resisting and standing firm in the Lord.

Let us not give the enemy a chance to destroy or curtail God's progress in us. "Be sober, be vigilant; because your adversary the devil walks about like a roaring lion, seeking whom he may devour" (1 Peter 5:8). Christians need "to be of sound mind; to exercise self-control."[4]

One part of the fruit of the Holy Spirit is self-control (Galatians 5:23). Thus, the presence of the Holy Spirit in one's life produces the sobriety needed to resist the enemy, who is always roaming around in search of whom to destroy.

And since the fight and the destruction are spiritual, there may be no immediate visible signs of destruction. Yet, with time, their words and actions will show whether the spirit of the enemy or the Spirit of God resides in the heart of every individual. The Bible tells us that we will know them by their fruit. Our loving God desires that all bear the Holy Spirit's fruit. That is a matter of life and death.

As long as we live in this world of sin, let us not relax our spiritual vigilance no matter how much success we gain in our ministries or walk with the Lord. The enemy does not respect any spiritual growth. He keeps trying all possible ways to bring down God's people, regardless of their spiritual growth. We are told, "Pray without ceasing" (1 Thessalonians 5:17). There is no rest on this side of heaven. Look at the facts explained in the following quote:

> Those who at Pentecost were endued with power from on high, were not thereby freed from further temptation and trial. As they witnessed for truth and righteousness, they were repeatedly assailed by the enemy of all truth, who sought to rob them of their Christian experience. They were compelled to strive with all their God-given powers to reach the measure of the stature of men and women in Christ Jesus. Daily they prayed for fresh supplies of grace, that they might reach higher and still higher toward perfection.

> Under the Holy Spirit's working even the weakest, by exercising faith in God, learned to improve their entrusted powers and to become sanctified, refined, and ennobled.[5]

Saints are never too far out of reach for Satan to tempt and distract them from the path of righteousness. Satan tried all he could to tempt Jesus and derail Him from His mission three times. If the devil had the audacity to tempt Jesus, we are never out of reach for him to tempt us. Ellen White states:

> Tests are placed all along the way from Earth to heaven. It is because of this that the road to heaven is called the narrow way. Character must be tested, else there would be many spurious Christians who would keep up a fair semblance of religion until their inclinations, their desire to have their own way, their pride and ambition, were crossed. When by the Lord's permission sharp trials come to them, their lack of genuine religion, of the meekness and lowliness of Christ, shows them to be in need of the work of the Holy Spirit.[6]

Without the help of the Holy Spirit, there can be no victory over the enemy.

My father told me about an exciting fighting technique of the Kamba people of Kenya. Many years ago, there used to be many regional wars involving the Kamba people. Cows were mostly the cause of the battles as one tribe drove away the cows of the other tribe. At the time, the primary weapons for the Kamba people were bows and arrows, which they shot dozens of meters away from the enemy.

With time, their enemies learned that the arrows would come straight from where the Kamba warriors were hiding. So, the enemies quickly identified the direction of the Kamba warriors and threw their spears or whatever weapons they had at the Kamba group. Then, the Kamba people devised a technique that confused the enemies. They learned how to shoot their arrows to the sky so that by the time these weapons reached the enemies, the arrows came down like rain from the sky. That way, the enemies did not know where the Kamba warriors were hiding. "Since we learned that technique," my father said, "our enemies never won the war against us again. As a result, they left our cows alone."

It is crucial to identify one's enemy and to know the enemy's fighting techniques. Satan, the only true enemy of God and His people, is very cunning. Without God's help, no human being can defeat Satan. No human being can discern the canning techniques of the devil. Only God's grace can help us. As promised in Genesis 3:15, Christ crushed the head of the serpent on the cross.

We often do not understand why God allows trials and temptations on the one hand, as in Job's case, and why He tests us as He did to Abraham on the other hand. In Job's case, we learn that God permits or allows evil to happen, even to His children; otherwise, we would treat our relationship with God as a charm to ward off evil. That would encourage a commercial relationship with God based on personal gain rather than love. In Abraham's case, we learn that God tests His people to develop their best qualities. His tests do not have an evil intent but a Divine purpose.

There are four reasons why people suffer. First, Satan is the archenemy of God's people here on Earth. He plants evil thoughts in people's minds, so they commit bad acts and cause undue harm to fellow human beings. Second, we suffer because of sin. As long as sin continues to exist, there will always be all kinds of suffering—disease, poverty, conflict, and abuses related to the misuse of power. Third, we suffer because of the irresponsibility of others. For example, a drunken driver runs through a red light and causes a car accident, resulting in injuries and fatalities. Fourth, we suffer because of our own foolishness. The wrong decisions we make often result in personal and public harm.

Trials and sufferings will come to every Christian on planet Earth. Scripture tells us to consider it all joy when we encounter various trials or temptations. God allows each of His children to experience trials and sufferings. These are meant to produce perseverance, which makes us spiritually "mature and complete" (James 1:2-4). Sometimes, these trials come in the form of pruning so we can "bear more fruit," as John 15:2 tells us. Every Christian needs the pruning process when God cuts off every part in us that may hinder us from yielding "much fruit" (John 15:5).

Christians are branches that remain connected to the Savior and are to bear the fruit of the Holy Spirit: "love, joy, peace, longsuffering, kindness, goodness, faithfulness, gentleness and self-control" (Galatians 5:22, 23). Without the presence of the Holy Spirit, there is no yielding of spiritual fruit.

Trials are tests that God allows to examine our spiritual standing and develop spiritual muscles in us. But God does not need to test us to know us. He already knows everything about us. He knows our thoughts and the motive behind every action. He knows the end from the beginning. So, trials reveal to us who we are, our need to depend on God, and our perpetual connection to Him. The struggles, prayers, and tears we may shed through these difficult times should always remind us that without God's grace, no human being is beyond sinning or failing. How do we get the help that we need to overcome?

CHAPTER 2

Receiving the Best Gifts

Suppose someone you love and trust wanted to give you a special gift, and the person told you, "Ask." What would you ask for? Scripture tells us, "Ask, and it will be given to you; seek, and you will find; knock, and it will be opened to you" (Mathew 7:7). Yet, the idea of asking is disagreeable to many. Many people do not accept help even when they need it, let alone ask for it. You may say, but many people are asking for handouts.

While some people are quick to ask for help, others detest the idea. Have you ever tried to help someone who needed whatever you were trying to offer? Then you were met with, "I'm good." Or, "I got it. Thanks." And that response does not have to come from a stranger. It could come from a colleague, neighbor, classmate, friend, or family member.

But isn't it comforting to meet all one's needs without seeking help from another person? And even when all the needs are not met, how many people want others to know that they are struggling in any way?

It is good that many people have things going on well in their lives—physically, socially, mentally, emotionally, and financially. Yet God our Creator knows that none of us is good or has got it because, spiritually, something is missing in every person's life. Thus, the Lord tells us:

> Ask, and it will be given to you; seek, and you will find; knock, and it will be opened to you. For everyone who asks receives, and he who seeks finds, and to him who knocks it will be opened. Or what man is there among you who, if his son asks for bread, will give him a stone? Or if he asks for a fish, will he give him a serpent? If you then, being evil, know how to give good gifts to your children, how much more will your Father who is in heaven give good things to those who ask Him! (Mathew 7:7-11).

What a loving and gracious heavenly Father we have! He wants us to ask for good things from Him. When we ask, we get the blessing. Let me explain this with a short story. A story is told about two men who lived before the era of cell phones and telephones in many African villages. In those days, if you needed to communicate with your neighbors, you went there or sent someone with the message. Two men visited the same neighbor to seek help. Each man arrived in his own time. When the first one arrived, he found the host and his family ready to eat breakfast. The host welcomed him into the house and invited him to eat with them. "We are about to take tea and mandazi." Mandazi is a bun made from wheat flour, sugar, and other ingredients. It is such a delicacy, especially in Kenya and Tanzania. The visitor took the offer and sat to enjoy tea and mandazi.

As they ate their breakfast, there was a knock on the door. "Come in," said the host. The person knocking requested to speak with the host at the door. So, the owner of the home went to the door. And after exchanging the usual greetings, the host welcomed him to join the family at the table. At that point, the second visitor made his request. He said, "I would like to join you at the table. But I first need your help. I want to borrow your ax to cut down trees on my farm. Please, let my young men use it. I will bring it back in the evening. If you give me the ax, I will hand it to the young men. Then I will come back and talk with you as we have tea and mandazi. Culturally, refusing the courtesy of food when offered was considered rude or even hostile.

The host gave him the ax and went back to the first visitor to continue with their talk while eating. When the host told the first visitor that he had to go out to get his ax and give it to the second visitor, the first visitor said, "I, too, came here to borrow your ax. I need it so badly in my field today." Sadly, the first visitor put food first before his real mission. The one who asked for the ax got it.

While we are free to ask for whatever we desire from God, He specifically assures us that He will give good things to those who ask Him. And unlike the kind neighbor with only one ax to give to his neighbors, God has plenty of good things to give to all His children who ask. What are the things the Lord promises to give those who ask Him? The Bible says: "If you then, though you are evil, know how to give good gifts to your children, how much more will your Father in heaven give the Holy Spirit to those who ask him!" (Luke 11:13 NIV). God wants us to ask for the Holy Spirit. "Good things" refers to the Holy Spirit, who dispenses spiritual gifts. However, God will also provide us with food, shelter, clothing, and other needs. More about these later. As we see in Scripture, the gift of the Holy Spirit is crucial in our lives as Christians. There is no victory over evil without the help of the Holy Spirit in our lives. Thus, there is no true Christianity without the Holy Spirit. And our gracious God assures us that He will give the Holy Spirit to those who ask.

Just like Jesus and God the Father, the Holy Spirit is God also. Peter rebuked Ananias for lying "to the Holy Spirit." He said, "You have not lied to men but to God" (Acts 5:3-

5). The Holy Spirit is a member of the Godhead. God dwells in us if we have the Holy Spirit in our hearts. The Holy Spirit reveals and teaches the things of God (1 Corinthians 2:10), and He is everywhere (omnipresent) at the same time (Psalm 139:3, 8). Omnipresence is one of God's divine attributes.

Moreover, "The Bible teaches that the Holy Spirit is a separate being. He is not simply an influence, an extension of the other members of the Godhead, such as the spirit of God or the spirit of Christ. Instead, He is the third person of the Godhead, a separate person who is as fully God as God the Father and God the Son" [1] The Bible sometimes uses expressions like the Spirit of God (Genesis 1:2), "The Spirit of the Lord, the Spirit of wisdom and understanding, the Spirit of counsel and might, the Spirit of knowledge and of the fear of the Lord "(Is. 11:2), and the Holy Spirit (2 Pet 1:21). Other designations are Helper (Jn 18:7), Intercessor (Rom 8:26), Spirit of God and Spirit of Christ (Rom 8:9). The expressions "Spirit of God" and "Spirit of Christ" do not imply that the Holy Spirit is subordinate to but an equal partner in the Godhead.

We can never overemphasize the vital role played by the Holy Spirit as the Comforter, Helper, Teacher, and Intercessor of God's people. He is the one who empowers God's people to resist trials and temptation. The Holy Spirit inspired the writers of the Bible, and He interprets the Bible for the human mind to know the Word of God. Because, as humans, we do not understand precisely how to talk to God, the Holy Spirit intercedes in our prayers, putting them the way they should be to reach God's ears. We read in Romans: "Likewise the Spirit also helps in our weaknesses. For we do not know what we should pray for as we ought, but the Spirit Himself makes intercession for us with groanings which cannot be uttered. Now He who searches the hearts knows what the mind of the Spirit is, because He makes intercession for the saints according to the will of God" (Romans 8: 26, 27). John says, "But the Helper, the Holy Spirit, whom the Father will send in My name, He will teach you all things, and bring to your remembrance all things that I said to you" (John 14:26).

While much can be said about the Holy Spirit, the most important thing for us to know is that the Holy Spirit is God. He is the third Person of the Godhead. And we need Him for our salvation. Scripture tells us, "Now if anyone does not have the Spirit of Christ, he is not His" (Romans 8:9). The three Persons of the Godhead work together; if we reject one, we reject God. Of course, Satan wants people to call themselves Christian but not believe what the Bible teaches about Christ or the Holy Spirit. We are in a spiritual battle, and Satan will use any weapon to give him victory.

On understanding the work of the Holy Spirit, Leroy Edwin Froom tells us: "Some have never understood it. It's like the Jews who would never understand Jesus."[2] Jesus promised to send the Holy Spirit to His disciples and all of us. The Holy Spirit came at Pentecost after Jesus left for heaven. The Helper glorifies Jesus Christ (John 16:7-15). Let us take a moment and look at the Godhead.

Jesus said whoever knows Him knows the Father (John 14:7). The Holy Spirit came from the Father through the prayers of Jesus (John 14:16). The Gospel of John gives us a perfect summary of who Jesus is, His role in creation, and His role in our salvation. We read:

> In the beginning was the Word, and the Word was with God, and the Word was God. He was in the beginning with God. All things were made through Him, and without Him nothing was made that was made. In Him was life, and the life was the light of men. And the light shines in the darkness, and the darkness did not comprehend it. He was in the world, and the world was made through Him, and the world did not know Him. He came to His own, and His own did not receive Him. But as many as received Him, to them He gave the right to become children of God, to those who believe in His name: who were born, not of blood, nor of the will of the flesh, nor of the will

of man, but of God. And the Word became flesh and dwelt among us, and we beheld His glory, the glory as of the only begotten of the Father, full of grace and truth. (John 1:1-4, 10-14)

So, Jesus is God. He was in the beginning with God, and He created everything. Jesus became flesh and lived among humans to save them. Those who accept Jesus as their Savior and obey Him as their Lord will receive eternal life (John 3:16; 14:15).

The Holy Spirit came to continue teaching and empowering people to surrender their lives to Jesus to escape eternal death. Ellen G. White says, "The Holy Spirit is Christ's representative, but divested of the personality of humanity, and independent thereof. Cumbered with humanity, Christ could not be in every place personally. Therefore, it was for their [the disciples'] interest that He should go to the Father and send the Spirit to be His successor on earth. No one could then have any advantage because of his location or his personal contact with Christ. By the Spirit the Saviour would be accessible to all."[3]

Indeed, the Holy Spirit is everywhere at the same time. No wonder Jesus told His disciples that the coming of the Helper would be to their advantage. Nonetheless, let us never think that Christ is far away in heaven. We read, "Jesus answered and said to him, 'If anyone loves Me, he will keep

My word; and My Father will love him, and We will come to him and make Our home with him'" (John 14:23). Yes, Jesus is in heaven, interceding for us. Yet, He and the Father dwell in the hearts of God's people through the Holy Spirit.

One of the attributes of God is omnipotence. Even though He is powerful and preeminent, He is also present. Before we sit with our Lord face to face, we may never fully understand these details about God being in heaven and, at the same time, dwelling among us and in us. We always need help understanding some things on this side of heaven. I don't know about you, but I want to ask Jesus these questions when I finally sit at His feet in heaven. We will have eternity and perfect brains to understand! Until then, Scripture tells us that we are saved by grace, and our faith in the Lord is necessary.

The Holy Spirit is a priceless gift. He dispenses spiritual gifts to us such as wisdom, knowledge, understanding, discernment, and every other precious gift that we need to be authentic Christians who serve God (1 Corinthians 12:4-11; Isaiah11:2; James 1:5). God's children are given whatever gifts they need to serve Him.

The blessing of the Holy Spirit is that He comes "as a counselor, sanctifier, guide, and witness."[4] He empowers God's people: "You shall receive power when the Holy Spirit has come upon you" (Acts 1:8). At Pentecost, the disciples received the Holy Spirit and were enabled to spread the gospel to the world. The same promise stands for us today. When we allow the Holy Spirit in our hearts, we receive the power to overcome sin and serve God.

The Holy Spirit teaches us to know God and teaches us about God's truths (John 14:26). Imagine going to school and having a good teacher to teach you everything you need to learn to succeed in life. While it can be such a blessing, there is no comparison between that teacher and the Holy Spirit, who teaches us all truth and prepares us for heaven. We receive God's love through the Holy Spirit (Romans 5:5). Our redemption is sealed through Him (Ephesians 4:30).

Indeed, one cannot be a Christian without the Holy Spirit. "But you are not in the flesh but in the Spirit, if indeed the Spirit of God dwells in you. Now if anyone does not have the Spirit of Christ, he is not His" (Romans 8:9). The presence of the Holy Spirit in one's heart is the indication that a person belongs to Christ.

Instead of seeking the Holy Spirit and Jesus Christ, many of us put our physical needs first. We think about food. We fast in tears for God to provide food and shelter for us. Of course, God knows that we need our basic needs met. And He does provide. He delivered the children of Israel from Egypt, and instead of settling them in the wilderness permanently, He took them to Canaan, a more productive land. In His ministry on earth, Christ did not only preach the good news and heal the sick; He also fed multitudes with bread and fish. Nonetheless, there is something more important to us than food, shelter, and physical healing. In the Gospel of Matthew, Jesus said, "But seek first the kingdom of God and His righteousness, and all these things shall be added to you" (Mathew 6:33). Will you seek first the kingdom of God and His righteousness in your life? How do we do that?

CHAPTER 3

The Overlooked Need

How possible is it to forget or overlook a need? Many conclude that it is not a need if it can be overlooked. There are needs that every person who prays can never ignore. If you are a prayer group member, consider the prayer requests that people send to the group regularly. Even if you are not a prayer group member, think about the needs for which you pray most. And even if you do not pray, think about the needs that concern you most.

I regularly write down lists of things for which I pray. After several years, I look over the lists, check the ones granted, and thank God for them. That is especially so for long-term requests. I also thank God for many things that He never granted me because, after many years, I look back and see the wisdom and grace of God for not giving me some things I persistently prayed for before. But asking for the Holy Spirit to fill my heart and the hearts of others was never on my prayer list for many years. Asking to be filled with the Holy Spirit is much overlooked by many Christians. Is praying to be filled with the Holy Spirit a need?

As humans, Maslow's hierarchy of needs is perhaps our primary default when we think about our needs. We realize the need to ask God for food, clothing, physical healing, shelter, protection from physical danger, money, and all other items. It is generally agreed that humans have five needs: physiological needs, safety, love and belonging, self-esteem, and self-actualization. The reasoning is that once the basic and the higher needs are met, a human being is in the best position in life. Of course, being filled with the Holy Spirit does not appear among Maslow's hierarchy of needs. And among Christians, this does not take the front banner as the greatest need.

Scripture tells us, "So then, those who are in the flesh cannot please God. But you are not in the flesh but in the Spirit, if indeed the Spirit of God dwells in you. Now if anyone does not have the Spirit of Christ, he is not His" (Romans 8:8, 9). According to God's Word, we need the Holy Spirit. The following story helps explain how the overlooked need of the Holy Spirit is inevitable in every Christian's life.

A certain woman enjoyed cakes that her friend baked regularly. She decided to learn how to bake them to enjoy them whenever she wanted. As an experienced baker, the friend wrote down the recipe and instructions. The recipe included wheat flour, milk, butter, sugar, eggs, and one teaspoonful of baking powder. When the woman who wanted to learn looked at the list of ingredients, she realized she had all the ingredients in her kitchen except the baking powder.

She also noted that while she needed other ingredients in larger quantities, she only needed a teaspoonful of baking powder. Her friend had told her that all the dry ingredients needed to be leveled but not heaped. So, she decided not to spend time going to the store for the baking powder. "After all," she told herself, "The cake needed a full cup of wheat flour and a full cup of milk and eggs." She reasoned that since the baking powder was such a small amount required for the cake, just one teaspoonful, she could bake her cake without it.

With her mind set on producing the best cake possible, she meticulously mixed all the ingredients according to her friend's instructions. She poured the mixture into a baking pan and put it in the oven, which had been set at the right temperature. She set the alarm to alert her when the cake was ready. After the specified time, the alarm went off. She opened the oven with all the excitement.

To her disappointment, the cake looked flat on the bottom of the baking pan. It did not rise as expected. It looked brown on the outside, but it was just at the original level of the mixture. By that time, she expected it to fill the baking pan. On cutting it, she realized that it did not cook well inside. She called her friend and expressed her disappointment and frustration. "What happened? Did you put all the ingredients I listed for you?" Her friend asked. "I did, except baking powder," she replied.

"You mean you did not put the baking powder?" the friend retorted in amazement. "Why?" she asked.

"Because it did not appear that a teaspoonful was crucial enough to make a difference in the ingredients. I thought the cake would come out just fine without that one ingredient. In any case, all the other ingredients were there," she explained. To that, her friend explained: "The lack of that one teaspoonful of baking powder messed up your cake. The baking powder makes the cake rise and cook well inside." She learned it the hard way.

Leroy Edwin Froom says, "Our great lack is not more earnestness, more importunity, more strength, more activity; it is our indifferent attitude toward the Holy Spirit. We are trying to render acceptable service in neglect of the one power by which it is accomplished."[1] Indeed, few people pray as they ought to, and fewer pray for the filling of the Holy Spirit.

Christians indeed have a measure of the Holy Spirit in them; otherwise, they would not have accepted Jesus as their Savior. But a Christian can have so little of the Holy Spirit and run empty like five of the ten virgins whose lamps were going out at a time of need (Matt 25:1-13). All ten waited until they dozed off when the bridegroom took a long time to return with his bride. But the wise virgins were ready for the groom because they had enough oil in their lamps. The foolish ones did not have oil in their lamps.

In Matthew 25:6-10 we read, "And at midnight a cry was heard: 'Behold, the bridegroom is coming; go out to meet him!' Then all those virgins arose and trimmed their lamps. And the foolish said to the wise, 'Give us some of your oil, for our lamps are going out.' But the wise answered, saying, '*No,* lest there should not be enough for us and you; but go rather to those who sell, and buy for yourselves.' And while they went to buy, the bridegroom came, and those who were ready went in with him to the wedding; and the door was shut."

The five foolish virgins missed the wedding, even though they waited for the bridegroom together with the other five.

One would think that all the ten virgins had enough oil to take them through the wedding process. In the Bible, oil represents the Holy Spirit, whom we all need for guidance toward salvation. The five foolish virgins were not hostile to the bridegroom; otherwise, they would not have waited for him that long together with the wise. They wanted to attend the wedding, but they needed to be wiser to carry extra oil for their lamps.

Jesus likened preparedness for the kingdom of heaven to the parable of the ten virgins. The five foolish virgins were partially and not fully prepared. Generally, oil represents the Holy Spirit in Scripture. Oil in lamps produces light so we can see our way through darkness. It will be costly for us as Christians if our dependence on the Holy Spirit is partial. Our spiritual lamps will go off when trials and temptations come our way. Trials and temptations are always around us. We cannot escape that fact. Things in life may seem to be going well and lull us to take our faith for granted and not rely on the Holy Spirit for guidance. The Holy Spirit comforts, energizes, teaches, and guides us. In our spiritual lives, the Holy Spirit is like the baking powder when baking the cake. Without Him in our hearts, we cannot grow and be victorious Christians. Without the Holy Spirit, we cannot have a genuine and loving relationship with God.

Froom explains the need to be filled with the Holy Spirit, stating: "Alas, many today have gone as far as the baptism of repentance, but no farther. They are honest, sincere, and obedient to the extent of their knowledge. But they are ignorant of the fuller, brighter, larger life. Whatever knowledge they have of the Holy Spirit is vague, indefinite, inadequate. His personality, power, and presence are not understood. They are largely ignorant of His program and provisions and are sadly barren of His fruits."[2] That is a terrible situation for anyone confessing to be a Christian. Yet, it does not have to be.

Every person who wants eternal life needs the infilling of the Holy Spirit. Moreover, spiritual leaders need the guidance of the Holy Spirit to know how to lead God's people according to God's will. If spiritual leaders allow false teaching to confuse them, that confusion will spread to their congregations. Let us pray and surrender fully to God so that He leads us into all truth. While many people are ignorant about the truths of the Bible and the need for the Holy Spirit, some have made up their minds that they do not want to know. Why? Because surrendering to God runs against the grain in their life.

I once faced a person who was spreading unbiblical teachings to church members. I, with two brothers from the church, sat down with him. After some time of Bible discussion, I realized that the person made deliberate statements. When we asked him where those statements were written in the Bible, he could not say. He refused to touch the Bible but continued making those same statements. We tried all we could for hours. But the person refused to use the Bible or to reason with us. We concluded that he did not want to know.

God does not force Himself or His teaching on anyone. But those who want to know Him will pray and ask for the Holy Spirit, the helper, comforter, and teacher. Jesus referred to Him as the Spirit of truth who guides us into "all truth" (John 16:13). We should pray for knowledge, wisdom, and discernment. We need daily filling of the Holy Spirit lest we fall prey to the devil, as Paul warned the Corinthians: "But even if our gospel is veiled, it is veiled to those who are perishing, whose minds the god of this age has blinded, who do not believe, lest the light of the gospel of the glory of Christ, who is the image of God, should shine on them" (2 Corinthians 4:3, 4).

Those who refuse to surrender fully to God will not have the power to resist the devil. The enemy will crowd their minds and make them blind to the teaching of Scripture. That is an unnecessary doom. Christ died to save us from the influence of Satan and death. The Holy Spirit came to provide perpetual power to overcome. Ellen G. White says:

"The Holy Spirit is the breath of spiritual life in the soul. The impartation of the Spirit is the impartation of the life of Christ. It imbues the receiver with the attributes of Christ."[3] Every true Christian needs the infilling of the Holy Spirit. When we ask for the infilling of the Holy Spirit, God will not withhold that from us. "If you then, being evil, know how to give good gifts to your children, how much more will *your* heavenly Father give the Holy Spirit to those who ask Him!" (Luke 11:13).

The question can be asked: How often should we ask for the filling of the Holy Spirit? Paul in Ephesians gives us a clue: "And do not be drunk with wine, in which is dissipation; but be filled with the Spirit" (Ephesians 5:18). The imperative, "be filled with the Spirit," is written in the present tense, which means that we are to be filled with the Holy Spirit continuously. On the same point, White says, "For the daily baptism of the Spirit, every worker should offer his petition to God."[4] We should allow ourselves to receive the baptism of the Holy Spirit daily. As Pentecost did not end with Acts 2, the Holy Spirit is not a one-time event or experience. It is ongoing. Let us pray and ask for the Holy Spirit's infilling daily.

CHAPTER 4

Receiving the Holy Spirit

Understanding the process of receiving the Holy Spirit is important because following the right path can make the difference between receiving and forfeiting the amazing gift. The Holy Spirit initiates the process of accepting Jesus as a Savior (Jn 16:8-10). Without the initiation of the Holy Spirit, no one can come to God or accept Jesus as Savior. Even after one repents and accepts Jesus, the Holy Spirit continues to comfort and enlighten the believer: "Then Peter said to them, '"Repent, and let every one of you be baptized in the name of Jesus Christ for the remission of sins; you shall receive the gift of the Holy Spirit'" (Acts 2:38).

To repent, one must receive the Holy Spirit since He is the one who convicts us of sin. When we confess our sins, we get baptized. At that point, God does not leave us alone, unattended. The Holy Spirit continues to work in our lives, leading us toward sanctification—Christian growth and maturity. Receiving the Holy Spirit is not a one-time event. It should happen daily. Ellen G. White says, "There is no limit to the usefulness of one who, by putting self aside, makes room for the working of the Holy Spirit upon his heart, and lives a life wholly consecrated to God."[1] Yielding one's heart to God, confessing sin, and turning away from it, is to live by the Spirit.

Froom brings up the same point: "There is an experience beyond and above the initial step by which the Holy Spirit first reveals sin, and begets a new life in the soul, and that is to be filled with the Spirit. For the lack of this, one's testimony is feeble and the spiritual life but partial."[2] Paul says, "Be filled with the Spirit" (Ephesians 5:18). This experience should continue until Jesus comes or until one sleeps in death.

When we obey God, we are cooperating with the work of the Holy Spirit in our hearts. The more we cooperate with the Holy Spirit, the more we cooperate with God. There is no separation between Jesus and the Holy Spirit in terms of who comes first and who comes last. Jesus said, "If you love Me, keep My commandments. And I will pray the Father, and He will give you another Helper, that He may abide with you forever—the Spirit of truth, whom the world cannot receive, because it neither sees Him nor knows Him; but you know Him, for He dwells with you and will be in you" (John 14:15-17).

Associated with receiving Christ and the Holy Spirit is the aspect of obedience, as we read, "And we are His witnesses to these things, and *so* also *is* the Holy Spirit whom God has given to those who obey Him" (Acts 5:32). Thus, obedience to God's Word, including His commandments, is evidence of receiving the Holy Spirit. It is an indication that someone is saved.

In giving the Holy Spirit, God is not partial. No one has a monopoly on the Holy Spirit, whether one is a believer or a non-believer. The Holy Spirit is available to all; but the difference is the willingness to open the door so He can come in. He is the instrument that keeps our love for God and our obedience to Him going every day of our lives. And as Jesus stated, our love for God is demonstrated through our obedience to His commandments.

Obeying God's Word opens one to receiving the Holy Spirit. The more we open ourselves to Him, the more we receive the Holy Spirit. Thus, we read: "During the patriarchal age the influence of the Holy Spirit had often been revealed in a marked manner, but never in its fullness. Now, in obedience to the word of the Saviour, the disciples offered their supplications for this gift, and in heaven Christ added His intercession. He claimed the gift of the Spirit, that He might pour it upon His people."[3]

Jesus said the world cannot receive the Holy Spirit because it does not know Him. Without the influence of the Holy Spirit, the world cannot have a loving relationship with God. On the other hand, those who give their lives to God get to know Him. They have Jesus as their Savior and Lord. These are the ones who receive the Holy Spirit. They live by the Spirit.

The Holy Spirit gives us the ability to do extraordinary things for Jesus. We are able to speak with conviction and boldness. The Holy Spirit becomes our defense when we are accused as ambassadors of Jesus Christ. Being filled with the Holy Spirit gives us the courage to face martyrdom when necessary. The Holy Spirit confirms Christ in our hearts, and we become His possession. Jesus said that whoever does not have the Holy Spirit is not His (Romans 8:9). Thus, having the Holy Spirit makes the difference between salvation and being lost. Having the Holy Spirit makes the difference between life and death. And in receiving the Holy Spirit, we can never overlook asking for the special gift. Scripture tells us to ask for the Holy Spirit. God is willing to give us.

The Word of God through the prophet Jeremiah was not only relevant to the Israelites. It still applies to us today.

"And you will seek Me and find *Me,* when you search for Me with all your heart" (Jeremiah 29:13). There is no better way of searching for God than allowing Christ to dwell in our hearts. We do that when we allow the Holy Spirit to dwell in us. Before Jesus left for heaven, He promised to send the Helper to the disciples. They sat in the upper room and prayed until they received the gift of the Holy Spirit.

Whoever is thirsty for the water of life gets filled. Jesus told the Samaritan woman, "Whoever drinks of this water will thirst again, but whoever drinks of the water that I shall give him will never thirst (John 4:13). What a great and comforting promise! That is what the Holy Spirit does in our lives. He is the spring of everlasting water in us. We already saw that the Holy Spirit makes the first move in entreating people to open their hearts to God. When they yield, He continues working on them. Jesus made it clear that only those who love Him will obey His Word. He also promised that He and the Father will dwell in the hearts of those who love Him (John 14:23). The Holy Spirit makes this possible.

Let us remember that God fills us with the Holy Spirit to enable us to witness for Him. All the power, wisdom, knowledge, discernment, teaching, and other gifts that the Holy Spirit bestows on God's people should be used to spread the gospel. The more we are led by the Spirit, the more He equips us to serve God.

The greatest blessing of all is being assured of God's presence in one's life. The Holy Spirit gives us that assurance. One of the crucial lessons Moses learned was the importance of God's presence among His people. Moses said: "Now therefore, I pray, if I have found grace in Your sight, show me now Your way, that I may know You and that I may find grace in Your sight. And consider that this nation is Your people. And He said, 'My Presence will go with you, and I will give you rest.' 'Then he said to Him, 'If Your Presence does not go with us, do not bring us up from here'" (Exodus 33:13-15). For Moses to tell God not to let him and the people of Israel go any further in their journey to the Promised Land without God's presence speaks volumes. How much do we value the presence of God in our lives?

God the Holy Spirit, God the Son, and God the Father work together in that they are always in agreement. When we pray for the indwelling of the Holy Spirit, we ask for God's presence in our lives; we pray for a very intimate relationship with God. We are asking God to be in us and us in Him. That is a deep God-human relationship.

By asking for the Holy Spirit, you ask for wisdom, knowledge, and all the needed grace to serve God successfully. Jesus promised, "He who believes in Me, as the Scripture has said, out of his heart will flow rivers of living water." 'But this He spoke concerning the Spirit, whom those believing in Him would receive; for the Holy Spirit was not yet given, because Jesus was not yet glorified'" (John 7:38, 39). Indeed, the presence of the Holy Spirit in one's life marks a true and faithful follower of Jesus. That person becomes a blessing in advancing the kingdom of God.

God has always wanted to be with His people. He instructed Moses to lead Israel to build a sanctuary so He could dwell among His people (Exodus 25:8). Jesus expressed the same desire before He left for heaven. He promised a Helper, the Holy Spirit, who would dwell not just among His people but in the hearts of the disciples and other believers. There was a need for Jesus to send the Holy Spirit to His followers. The Helper is equally needed today. Correctly, Pavel Goia and Kelly Mowrer said: "Salvation is Jesus Christ living in us through His Holy Spirit. "[4]

The blessing of God's presence cannot be fully exhausted, let alone in this book. When we get to heaven, we will fully understand it and experience it even more. Nonetheless, everything we need to know about God and our salvation in this life is revealed to us in Scripture. We read one of the incredible blessings of allowing God's presence in our lives in Ezekiel 36:26, 27: "I will give you a new heart and put a new spirit within you; I will take the heart of stone out of your flesh and give you a heart of flesh. I will put My Spirit within you and cause you to walk in My statutes, and you will keep My judgments and do them." What a blessing!

God is always ready to give a new heart to whoever is willing to receive it. That new heart comes with Jesus Christ, the Savior, and it involves the ministry of the Holy Spirit, who entreats us to accept the Savior. Just reread the following sentence and think about it. "I will put My Spirit within you and cause you to walk in My statutes, and you will keep My judgments and do them." God desires to maintain a long-lasting relationship with whoever wants it. His love and our obedience sustain that relationship.

In the book of Acts, we read that God was present in the ministry of Jesus here on earth, "how God anointed Jesus of Nazareth with the Holy Spirit and with power, who went about doing good and healing all who were oppressed by the devil, for God was with Him" (Acts 10:38). The Savior received the anointing of the Holy Spirit and power from above. The ministry of the Holy Spirit is crucial to our salvation. Yet, there are not many sermons about Him. The importance of the duties of the Holy Spirit in our lives is not a surprise. In any case, He is the third Person of the Godhead. Each one plays an indispensable role in our salvation; it has been so from the beginning and will continue to the end.

God is so loving that He offered His son to die for us. And that same God, who is so merciful, all-knowing, all-powerful, wants to dwell in us. King David danced joyfully because the Ark of the Covenant was coming to Jerusalem. All the Israelites and David were filled with joy and praise. They offered sacrifices to God. The ark of the covenant was a symbol of God among them. Hence, the Israelites were so happy and comforted to have the ark with them. When we have the Holy Spirit, we do not only have God with us. We have God with us and in us.

If we delight ourselves in the Lord, we seek His presence daily. But we cannot seek or obey Him unless the Holy Spirit leads us. And the Holy Spirit will not lead us unless we have Him in us. How do we know that we have the presence of God in us? God's presence in us is manifested by the presence of the Holy Spirit, who produces His fruit in God's people. "The fruit of the Spirit is love, joy, peace, longsuffering, kindness, goodness, faithfulness, gentleness, self-control" (Galatians 5:22,23).

God's presence is universal, unlike the presence of our loved ones, which circumstances can limit. There are places and times when family members and friends cannot come to see us in the hospital or behind bars. They may give us all types of support in life, but their full presence is restricted in many situations. But the Holy Spirit is with God's people all the time, everywhere they go. "O, how we need the divine presence! For the baptism of the Holy Spirit every worker should be breathing out his prayer to God. "[5] Let us ask for the filling of the Holy Spirit. Froom states, "There is an experience beyond and above the initial step by which the Holy Spirit first reveals sin and begets a new life in the soul, and that is to be filled with the Spirit. For the lack of this, one's testimony is feeble and the spiritual life but partial."[6] No wonder Scripture tells us, "Be filled with the Spirit" (Ephesians 5:18). Pray for the filling of the Holy Spirit, will you?

CHAPTER 5

Seeking God Diligently

One of the most comforting promises in the Bible reads, "You will seek Me and find Me, when you search for Me with all your heart" (Jeremiah 29:13, NIV). The children of Israel were in captivity in Babylon when they were given this promise through the prophet Jeremiah. It gave them hope to know that God still loved them. Yes, they had sinned and refused to repent when they were given the chance. But God had not given up on them. If they turned their hearts to the Lord, they would find Him. God is always there for His people.

Before we go deeper into seeking the Lord, let us remember that God goes after the sinner first. He pursues the lost way before they realize their condition. That is why God gave His Son to die for the world. As a result, "whoever believes in Him" will get eternal life (John 3:16). God never changes. He remains loving, kind, and faithful. The Israelites were given the same offer of salvation as we are today. God delivered them from their captivity in Egypt. They knew Him, but they chose to go contrary to His will. God did not reject His people. He accepted them the many times they repented.

Seeking God diligently will only happen if we obey what Jesus said in Mathew 22:37: "You shall love the LORD your God with all your heart, with all your soul, and with all your mind." To seek the Lord with all our hearts calls for total surrender. It also requires the willingness to do God's will. Submission to God's instructions is part of our seeking God.

Total surrender to God requires admission of sin, repentance, confession, accepting God's forgiveness, and living a life of faith, love, and hope. It means learning to trust God in everything He says. Seeking God must involve worshiping Him in "spirit and in truth." That refers to "all sincerity, with the highest faculties of the mind and emotions, applying the principles of the truth to the heart "[1] This means immersing ourselves in studying His Word. That is when God speaks to us directly. When He does, we must learn to develop the patience to listen to what His Word says, even when it confronts our habits and practices.

Furthermore, God's Word is our shield. Paul tells us to put on "the sword of the Spirit, which is the word of God," which is the "whole armor of God" (Ephesians 6:13, 17). Ellen White tells us, "There is nothing more calculated to energize the mind and strengthen the intellect than the study of the word of God. No other book is so potent to elevate the thoughts, to give vigor to the faculties, as the broad, ennobling truths of the Bible. If God's word were studied as it should be, men would have a breadth of mind, a nobility of character, and a stability of purpose that are rarely seen in these times. The search for truth will reward the seeker at every turn, and each discovery will open up richer fields for his investigation."[2]

Seeking God diligently also means seeking Him through prayer. Prayer is us talking to God. Many times, when we pray, we do not get what we want or what we are asking for. God has several ways of responding to our prayers. He may say yes, no, or wait. These responses may be clear in our minds, but we often do not know His will. The Bible says, "Rejoice always, pray without ceasing, in everything give thanks; for this is the will of God in Christ Jesus for you" (1 Thessalonians 5:16- 18). "Men always ought to pray and not lose heart" (Luke 18:1). "The LORD is near to all who call on him, to all who call on him in truth" (Psalm 145:18). All these verses encourage us to pray and keep on praying faithfully.

The Kamba people of Kenya value their elders, for they are associated with wisdom and knowledge. So, the Kamba people have a saying, "Utui wi atumia ndunyaa," meaning that a village where elders reside never experiences drought. In this saying, drought does not only refer to lack of literal rain. It also refers to any situation that calls for "wisdom and knowledge" that guides people to safety and prosperity. So, people are blessed by the presence of the elders in the village. God is more than all the world's elders put together. He has unfathomable wisdom in everything. He calls into existence anything He desires. Hence, seeking God is seeking the best both in this life and in the life to come. We will not lack anything when we put God at the center of our lives. He will always make sure that our needs are met.

Through prayer, we maintain our connection with God. Through prayer, we respond to His call. The Holy Spirit makes all this possible when we pray. God wants us to continually ask, seek, and knock (Mathew 7:7). This is why Jesus told a parable about a widow who persistently approached a judge: "There was in a certain city a judge who did not fear God nor regard man. Now there was a widow in that city; and she came to him, saying, 'Get justice for me from my adversary.' And he would not for a while; but afterward he said within himself, 'Though I do not fear God nor regard man, yet because this widow troubles me I will avenge her, lest by her continual coming she weary me.'" (Luke 18:1-5)

Somebody said the door to God is marked "PUSH" (**P**ray **U**ntil **S**omething **H**appens). This persistence will only happen if one places much value on whatever is sought. For nine years, I prayed for the reunion of my family, which had been separated by distance between two continents. And for those nine years, a day hardly passed without me asking God to reunite my family. God performed miracles, and what seemed impossible came to pass.

People do not persist in seeking and asking for help from God if they do not have trust and faith in Him. We need to trust in God's faithfulness, kindness, and ability to provide whatever we ask of Him. Also, we need to be the kind of Christians He wants us to be.

Indeed, when we seek God and allow Him into our hearts, He will surely come in. The *Seventh-day Bible Commentary* on the book of Mathew states, "Those who ask will not be disappointed. God is not sparing with the gifts of heaven; He does not deal with men in the way they deal with one another, but is gracious and merciful."[3] So we will not seek our heavenly Father in vain. We will not ask for God's presence in our lives in vain. We will not cry for God's guidance and power in our lives in vain. He is generous with the gifts of heaven. Praise be His name forever.

CHAPTER 6

The Audacity to Ask

God permits His children to approach Him with confidence. Scripture tells us: "Seeing then that we have a great High Priest who has passed through the heavens, Jesus the Son of God, let us hold fast our confession. For we do not have a High Priest who cannot sympathize with our weaknesses, but was in all points tempted as we are, yet without sin. Let us therefore come boldly to the throne of grace, that we may obtain mercy and find grace to help in time of need" (Hebrews 4:14-16). Jesus understands what we go through here on earth, and He sympathizes with us. The Word of God calls God's people to go to His throne of mercy confidently.

Those who surrender their lives to the Lord can approach God's throne daily without fear. They also allow the Holy

Spirit to fill them and use them in the salvation of others. In the face of difficulties, they rely on God, praying firmly and boldly for God to make a way. E. M. Bounds states, "Heaven has listening ears only for the wholehearted and the deeply earnest. Energy, courage, and perseverance must back the prayers that heaven respects and that God hears."[1] When the Israelites murmured in the wilderness, they lost an opportunity to show their courage and faith in God.

The Holy Spirit gives the power that moves God's people to pray boldly. They ask for whatever the Holy Spirit impresses on their minds. We have plenty of such in the Bible. Elisha asked for the double portion of Elijah's spirit. We read, "And so it was, when they had crossed over, that Elijah said to Elisha, 'Ask! What may I do for you, before I am taken away from you?' Elisha said, 'Please let a double portion of your spirit be upon me'" (2 Kings 2:9). Talk about the audacity to ask!

Another good example of asking is Solomon, who asked for wisdom. Real wisdom comes from God (Proverbs 2:6). Up to this day, the wisdom of Solomon amazes us. God's people must have the courage to ask for the best from their heavenly Father.

A group of young men and women worked in a certain organization. Among them was a young woman who could easily win many beauty contests. Above all, she loved Jesus.

She also had a very handsome, educated fiancé outside the organization. Then, her organization hired a professional young man who spotted the beautiful young woman. After some time, this new hire inquired about the beautiful young woman from other young men. "That one you cannot get. She is engaged to someone you cannot compete with," a colleague told the new hire. Nonetheless, the new hire befriended the young woman to learn more about her directly. After some time, he realized that the lady was not engaged anymore. For reasons known between her and her fiancé, she had decided to break the engagement and end the relationship without saying a word to other people.

Then, she fell in love with this new hire. A few months into their relationship, the young lady realized that the new colleague was the kind of person she wanted for a husband. Similarly, the young man realized that the young lady was not just beautiful on the outside but on the inside, too. He saw the kind of woman he wanted for a wife in her. Their relationship developed to a point where, months later, he proposed. And she said, "Yes."

When they got engaged, the other young men in the organization could not believe it. They were surprised that he got the girl they thought was beyond reach. He asked, and she said yes, and a beautiful wedding followed. We need to ask!

God wants to give us the best and tells us to ask. Let us do it with confidence. Once we surrender to God and get into a loving relationship with Him, we can ask for big things from Him. He is the Lord of the universe. Nothing is too hard for Him. In the lives of His people, the Lord conquers fear and doubt. He promises to honor those who humble themselves to Him (1 Peter 5:6).

White says, "The Lord gives us the privilege of seeking Him individually in earnest prayer, of unburdening our souls to Him, keeping nothing from Him who has invited us, 'Come unto Me, all ye that labor and are heavy-laden, and I will give you rest.' Oh, how grateful we should be that Jesus is willing and able to bear all our infirmities and strengthen and heal all our diseases if it will be for our good and for His glory."[2] Throughout our lives, we will face challenging situations. Faith and trust in God will give us the confidence to ask God to carry us over the roadblocks and make a way. God honors faith. If whatever we ask is good according to His plans and purposes for our lives, He will perform miracles and provide. Let us ask for whatever we need in our lives in faith, allowing His will to be done in all situations.

"Now this is the confidence that we have in Him, that if we ask anything according to His will, He hears us" (1 John 5:14). God is the best parent in the universe. He is the most responsible parent ever, and it is common knowledge that loving and responsible parents do not give everything a child asks. Many times, children ask for things that parents know will not be good for them. Other times, children ask for things that are not the best. So, parents give something better instead of providing what the child asks for. That is our God. We must trust Him enough to know He will give us the best in any situation. Remember, the best can be packaged in disguise. It may even be painful initially. But in the end, it can be much better than what may initially look like a blessing.

On October 13, 2022, I read a fascinating article online in which a politician requested another to endorse him to win an election in one of the states in America. The news said that both politicians were antagonists in some issues and that the one asking for help had severally refused to support the other. The story was long, at some point detailing a situation of strong "dramatic tension." Interestingly, it went on to say that "audacity was in abundant supply." As a reader, I could guess the results of the asking for support.

Then I thought God wants us to master all the audacity we can afford and ask for big things from Him. Imagine asking the God of the universe to dwell in you. Remember, this is the God who called the universe into existence. Jesus encouraged the same audacity in Luke 11:5-8, where someone in need of bread from his friend at night would knock on the door until he got it, refusing all excuses from the friend. The encouraging thing with God is that no matter your past failures, He wants you to come to Him as you are.

Jesus died for us and paid all debt for our sins. If we accept Christ's offer and give our lives to Him, Satan has nothing to claim on us. There is forgiveness of sin and the power to live righteous lives to God's glory. Jesus did not only die for our sins but also prays for us. He intercedes for us in heaven right now. No wonder Christ promised that whatever we ask in His name, the Father will do it (John 14:13). Also, the Holy Spirit intercedes for us here on earth. He dwells in our hearts to lead us in paths of righteousness. What a blessing! Our part is to cooperate with the Holy Spirit. That allows us to develop a relationship with God. It is that relationship that gives us the courage to approach God with confidence. Will you pray for grace to enter a loving relationship with God?

CHAPTER 7

The Role of Faith in Asking

Faith is a major prerequisite in asking and receiving whatever we need from God. We can never over-emphasize the importance of faith in claiming God's promises to us. Scripture tells us, "Therefore I say to you, whatever things you ask when you pray, believe that you receive them, and you will have them" (Mark 11:24). Unless we have faith that God is good, merciful, faithful, and able to provide whatever we need, we will not ask. And if we do, it will not be the kind of prayer God honors. We need to have faith in God and trust that He will keep His promises to us. But what exactly is faith?

When we were at school as students, we used to play the game of standing with a chair behind us. Behind the chair would be someone holding the chair and giving you instructions to sit or stand. You had to follow instructions to stand or sit on the chair. After several performances, your mind got used to the fact that there was a chair to sit on. But at some point, the person holding the chair pulled the chair back while instructing you to sit on it. At that point, you found yourself landing on the floor. After such an experience, you never trusted the instructions you were given. The person giving the instructions was deemed unreliable. Faith is like sitting on the chair and knowing that God will not pull the chair behind you because He is reliable and trustworthy. Faith is like sitting on the chair and knowing it is strong enough to hold you. Hebrews 11:1 says, "Now faith is the substance of things hoped for, the evidence of things not seen." Faith is a strong assurance that God will deliver all He promises: salvation, sustenance, protection, and eternal life. Faith is the backbone of our Christian life. Without it, our Christianity crumbles down.

Faith refers to trust, confidence, faithfulness, and reliability. The *Seventh-day Bible Commentary* on the book of Hebrews says that faith has two "shades of meaning that are closely interwoven throughout the chapter, for in each instance of faith cited, an attitude of faith led to faithful deeds. Emphasis is on faithful deeds"[1] So, if we have faith in God, we will show it in our actions. Hebrews 11 presents us with various heroes who took bold steps with strong faith and trust that God would come through. This chapter never ceases to amaze me.

The wonders accomplished in the lives of the people of God through faith are incredible. For instance, Abel's sacrifice was accepted while Cain's was rejected. Faith made the difference. Then there is the case of Enock, who did not experience death like other humans because God took him to heaven. The Bible says that while Enoch lived on earth, he pleased God. Hebrews 11:6, "But without faith *it is* impossible to please *Him,* for he who comes to God must believe that He is, and *that* He is a rewarder of those who diligently seek Him." Yes, indeed, God rewards faith.

By faith, Moses chose to identify with the Israelites, enslaved people, instead of staying in the palace as the grandson of the Pharaoh of Egypt. Moses had deep faith that God would lead the children of Israel to the Promised Land. Imagine the panic the Israelites had in front of the Red Sea as Pharaoh was in hot pursuit of them! They panicked and murmured while Moses pointed them to the faithfulness and power of God (Exodus 14).

Think of Joseph, Egypt's prime minister, a powerful country at the time. Joseph had so much faith in God that he instructed the Israelites to take his bones with them when the time came to leave Egypt. Joseph believed that God would bring His people out of Egypt (Hebrews 11:22) to the land of promise. That is what faith in the goodness and faithfulness of God looks like.

All the people we read about in Hebrews 11 were humans like us. Yet, they had authentic faith in God, which He rewarded. Jesus said everything will be possible for those who believe (Mark 9:23).

A strong and loving relationship with God will yield trust, persistent prayer, obedience, and service to God, even when promises are delayed. Otherwise, James tells us, "Thus also faith by itself, if it does not have works, is dead," and that Abraham demonstrated his faith in God when "he offered Isaac his son on the altar" (James 2:17, 21). Yes, faith must be genuine for it to work.

From Genesis to Revelation, we see that God honored faith. We are given plenty of examples of people who exercised faith in God. One of them was Noah. "By faith Noah, being divinely warned of things not yet seen, moved with godly fear, prepared an ark for the saving of his household, by which he condemned the world and became heir of the righteousness which is according to faith" (Hebrews 11:7). Noah had never seen rain before, let alone floods enough to cover mountains. But he believed and obeyed when God told him to build the ark as a hiding place from rain.

Noah's faith in God was so strong that he believed that it would rain, and the rain would destroy the world even though it had never rained before. And for 120 years, Noah embarked on an incredible project of building the ark amidst much ridicule from the people of his time. As a result, only his family of eight was saved. And now he is honored as the heir of the righteousness that comes by faith.

Abraham was instructed to leave his land of Ur of the Chaldees to go to an unknown place that God would show him. By faith, Abraham left in obedience to God. Later, we see him willing to sacrifice his only son, Isaac, in obedience to God's instruction (Genesis 22). Abraham passed the test. The Bible's stories of Abraham, Noah, and many others show us what faith in God is like. Joshua prayed, and the sun stood still so he and the Israelites could fight and defeat their enemies (Joshua 10:12,13).

Throughout His ministry on earth, Jesus honored faith. The Savior often said, "Your faith has made you whole." Or "your faith has made you well," depending on the Bible translation you read. He said these words to people whom He healed from diseases and to others whom He set free from the bonds of Satan. The story of the woman healed by touching the hem of Jesus' garment in Mark 5 is an example of a big reward for faith.

The Mission Venture Ministries explains the nature of faith well. It says that faith is "the assurance that the things revealed and promised in the Word are true, even though unseen, and gives the believer a conviction that what he expects in faith will come to pass."[2] Of all the Israelites who left Egypt, only Caleb and Joshua made it to the promised land. A whole generation of the Israelites perished in the wilderness. They were unable to enter the Promised Land because of their unbelief. In the same way, faith is needed to enter heaven. Whoever believes in the Savior will be saved.

Scripture tells us how to get faith. It says, "So then faith comes by hearing, and hearing by the word of God" (Romans 10:17). We must study God's Word for our faith to grow. Also, faith grows when we associate with mature Christians and attend church services regularly.

I came to America on a religious visa (R-1 visa) as a missionary teacher after a Christian school offered me a job. A few months into the position, I engaged an immigration attorney to guide me in processing a green card. Halfway through the process, the attorney told me that the R-1 visa would unlikely give me a green card. I told the attorney that I was asking for the document from God. That made no sense to him. "You will lose your money for nothing," the attorney told me. But I insisted.

I prayed and asked God for the green card, and I was convinced He would give it to me. I needed to process the document to bring my children over. I had been praying for God to make a way to reunite my family. My husband was in Texas at the time. I got the job in Tennessee, and the children were in Kenya, a situation I refused to accept. I prayed and believed that God would make a way. When my attorney tried to advise me to drop the pursuit of my green card halfway through, I told him: "Here is your fee. Do the job and give it your best shot. I am asking for the document from God. Just process the application."

To make the long story short, I got the green card within a very short time, and I got it when many R-1 visa holders had been turned down in their pursuit of a US green card. My attorney had valid reasons to advise me to keep my money. I insisted on the pursuit because I had such deep faith and trust that God would give me the green card. My faith and trust in God gave me the courage to reject my attorney's advice to quit. I am happy that God's grace fixed my eyes on His goodness. As a result, my children got their green cards, and the family was reunited after many years of painful separation because of distance. Whatever we need from our God, let us ask in faith, and God will give more than we can ever imagine.

CHAPTER 8

Claiming God's Promises

The Bible contains all kinds of promises from God. Over and over, God tells us that He keeps His Word. God delivered every single promise He made in the past. He promised Abraham a son. And even though his wife, Sarah, was barren and beyond child-bearing age, she became pregnant and gave birth to Isaac (Genesis 21:1-7).

The Lord promised the beautiful fertile land of Canaan to the children of Israel. And even though they were slaves with no ammunition or war experience, God gave them the land, as He had promised (Genesis 12:7; Joshua 1-24).

Out of love, God has given His people promises that cover every situation, both in this life and in the life to come. We are also given detailed instructions on how to claim the promises successfully. We read, "Therefore do not worry, saying, 'What shall we eat?' or 'What shall we drink?' or 'What shall we wear?' For after all these things, the Gentiles seek. For your heavenly Father knows that you need all these things. But seek first the kingdom of God and His righteousness, and all these things shall be added to you" (Mathew 6: 31-33). Nothing is more comforting than asking God to honor His Word in your life. He already knows all our needs and promises to provide for them all. But we need to put Him first.

In 1996, I experienced one of the greatest disappointments in my life. So, I decided to read the Bible and seek answers from God. In less than two months, I read the Bible from cover to cover for the first time. I read every word and every sentence from Genesis to Revelation. As I read, I underlined every verse that spoke to my situation. And I can tell you, thousands of great promises from our faithful God are waiting for us to claim in faith. Some scholars suggest there are between 7,000 and 8,000 promises in the Bible. That's a lot.

Jesus said, "If you abide in Me, and My words abide in you, you will ask what you desire, and it shall be done for you" (John 15:7). What a promise! To abide in Christ means that we are His disciples, willing to learn from Him and obey His instructions. Thus, we must surrender to Him fully and remain surrendered. And if His Word abides in us, it means we obey it, which will gradually transform us to be like Him. We can ask for whatever we desire from the Lord and trust Him enough to accept His will in every request.

Here is another promise: "If we confess our sins, He is faithful and just to forgive us our sins and to cleanse us from all unrighteousness" (1 John 1:9). Every human being needs forgiveness from sin. "If we say that we have no sin, we deceive ourselves, and the truth is not in us" (1 John 1:8). God created us, so He knows us better than we know ourselves. He tells us that there is no eternal life without forgiveness of sin. He promises to forgive our sins if we confess them. Once we confess our sins and ask for forgiveness, we must believe that our sins are forgiven.

Furthermore, we read, "And my God shall supply all your need according to His riches in glory by Christ Jesus" (Philippians 4:19). The greatest need for every human being is Jesus. He is the only Savior we will ever have in this world. When we have Jesus, the rest of God's blessings come with it.

Isaiah 26:3 tells us, "You will keep him in perfect peace, Whose mind *is* stayed *on You,* Because he trusts in You." God's promise is that He will keep His people in perfect peace because they trust Him. The need for peace does not care about age, race, gender, or social class. Children and seniors all need peace.

Remember that our heavenly Father promises to give His people every good thing. He promises to meet every need, including food, shelter, clothing, rest, strength, wisdom, protection, victory over evil, perpetual connection with Him, and everlasting life. Let us study the Bible and identify and claim these promises in faith. Over and over, Scripture tells us to pray, to ask, to trust, to remain in God, to put Him first, and then, He will supply all our needs. And when there is a delay or even a complete failure to get the exact things that we ask from God, let us always remember that "All things work together for good to those who love God, to those who are the called according to *His* purpose" (Romans 8:28). Even the disappointments that God allows are meant for good. God works through any situation in which He allows His children to bring out good results.

The Holy Spirit gives us the wisdom to seek first the kingdom of God and His righteousness. When we do, it becomes God's responsibility to know what we need and to give us what we need at the appropriate time.

God's promises are obtained by faith through the working of the Holy Spirit on our behalf. Hence, we need to claim the gift of the Holy Spirit. And let us remember, "It is not bestowed apart from prayer. 'When they had prayed, the place was shaken… and they were all filled with the Holy Ghost.'"[1] In His mercy, God gives His people the grace to believe and trust in Him.

One of my favorite promises in Scripture is in the last book of the Bible. "He who testifies to these things says, 'Surely I am coming quickly.' Amen. Even so, come, Lord Jesus!" (Revelation 22:20). No matter what happens in this life, Jesus Christ is coming quickly.

CHAPTER 9

Allowing God to Transform Your Desires

Looking at the title of this chapter, someone may ask: Why should God want to transform our desires? That is the question we will answer in this chapter. Desire has several definitions; here is one of them: "A passion excited by the love of an object, or uneasiness at the want of it, and directed to its attainment or possession."[1] In other words, a desire is a deep longing for something.

God created us with the capacity to desire. "Delight yourself also in the Lord, And He shall give you the desires of your heart" (Psalm 37:4). The nature of the desire (good or evil) depends on the desired object. When God created Adam and Eve, He addressed the issue of desire by giving them instructions on what to eat and what not to eat. Then the serpent went to Eve and asked, "Has God indeed said, 'You shall not eat of every tree of the garden'?" (Genesis 3:1). Eve stated God's commandment to the serpent that the humans were not supposed to eat the fruit of the tree in the middle of the garden, or else, they would die. But the serpent lied to Eve, "You will not surely die. For God knows that in the day you eat of it your eyes will be opened, and you will be like God, knowing good and evil. So when the woman saw that the tree *was* good for food, that it *was* pleasant to the eyes, and a tree desirable to make *one* wise, she took of its fruit and ate" (Genesis 3:4-6). The humans failed the test because of desire.

Galatians 5:16 gives us the solution: "So I say, walk by the Spirit, and you will not gratify the desires of the flesh" (Galatians 5:16 NIV). All human beings are under the control of the desires of the flesh unless they allow the Holy Spirit to take over those natural passions. The Holy Spirit installs the Lordship of Jesus in our lives. Putting on Christ means transformation into a new way of life.

David said, "I desire to do your will, my God your law is within my heart." (Psalm 40:8). And look at God's testimony about David: "He raised up for them David as king, to whom also He gave testimony and said, 'I have found David the *son* of Jesse, a man after My *own* heart, who will do all My will

(Acts 13:22).'" That should be the attitude of every Christian, to seek God with all one's heart. When people love and trust God, their desires align with God's will. Then, God honors their prayers. When they seek Him, they find Him. He gives His people the desires of their hearts, according to His will. We have many examples in the Bible.

Hannah found herself in a situation of barrenness. Her counterpart, Peninnah, had children and taunted Hannah mercilessly. Hannah had an intense desire to have a son. And of all the options she could have pursued, she chose to trust God and turn over her troubles to Him. It was such a bad situation for Hannah. Yet, instead of hanging herself like Judas, she trusted God with her problems.

Even though Hannah's burden was so heavy, I see faith and trust in her. She knew that God cared enough to listen to her and that He could see deep down in her heart. God honored her prayer. Scripture says, "Hannah conceived and bore a son, and called his name Samuel, saying, 'Because I have asked for him from the Lord'" (1 Samuel 1:20). God blessed Hannah with the son, Samuel, who became a great prophet on behalf of the people of Israel.

We worship the same God who saw Hannah's tears. You may not need a child, but as humans, we have all sorts of needs we want met. Many people desire to be healed spiritually, physically, emotionally, and in other ways. Others desire God's intervention in their social and financial matters.

Let us trust God with our needs and the desires of our hearts and be ready to accept His response to our prayers. Whether the answer is Yes, No, or Wait, the Lord knows what is best for us in every situation. He is faithful and merciful enough to give us the best, even if it is not what we request from Him. His Word tells us, "Be anxious for nothing, but in everything by prayer and supplication, with thanksgiving, let your requests be made known to God; and the peace of God, which surpasses all understanding, will guard your hearts and minds through Christ Jesus" (Philippians 4:6, 7). God is willing to supply all our needs. And He is also willing and able to give us the desires of our hearts.

Without faith in the goodness of God, our prayers are just noise that God does not honor. White says,

> There are few who rightly appreciate or improve the precious privilege of prayer. We should go to Jesus and tell Him all our needs. We may bring Him our little cares and perplexities as well as our greater troubles. Whatever arises to disturb or distress us, we should take it to the Lord in prayer. When we feel that we need the presence of Christ at every step, Satan will have little opportunity to intrude his temptations.

> It is his studied effort to keep us away from our best and most sympathizing friend. We should make no one our confidant but Jesus. We can safely commune with Him of all that is in our hearts.[2]

Scripture gives various requirements that we need to meet for God to grant us the things we ask for—praying in the name of Jesus (John 14:13), agreeing (Mathew 18:19), and obeying Him. Moreover, we read, "Whatever we ask we receive from Him, because we keep His commandments and do those things that are pleasing in His sight" (1 John 3:22).

Many times, we ask for things that we believe are good. So, when we do not receive them, we get confused and even discouraged. Let us always remember to ask God's will to be done in every situation. According to our judgment, what we ask at a particular time may be good. But God may want to give us something better. Or we may be asking for a blessing we cannot handle at the moment. Sometimes, the timing may not be suitable for reasons best known to God alone. For example, there was a time when Paul wanted to take the gospel to Asia. But the Holy Spirit told him not to go there at the time (Acts 16:6,7). Of course, God wants all people to be saved. But His work must be done at His timing.

The Lord assures us that He has good plans for us. He wants us to prosper. So, when we surrender ourselves fully in His hands and pray according to His Word but fail to get whatever we ask, let us not despair. Let us continue praying for God's will to be done in our lives. The Holy Spirit will reveal to us what to do in every situation. Do we need to continue praying for that job, or do we need to move on to other opportunities? God will give us the wisdom to know His will, especially on petitions not concerning salvation.

When we put God first in our lives, He becomes our Shepherd. Then He makes sure that we lack nothing. Whether we are praying for spiritual matters or provisions in this life, faith and trust in God are crucial.

Let us learn a lesson from Elijah. The man of God prayed, and there was no rain for three and a half years. Afterward, he prayed, and it rained to the blessing of humanity and other inhabitants of the earth (James 5:16-18). We can learn so much from Elijah's prayer. Seven times, he prayed, checked for the rain, and returned to pray until it came. Here, we see persistence in prayer. But how was he able to do that a whole seven times? Elijah had a relationship with God. Elijah had faith that God would answer his prayer to His glory. Unless we have faith and trust in God's goodness and faithfulness to keep His promises to us, we will not trust Him with our needs.

The Holy Spirit plays a crucial role in our requests to God. As C.S. Lewis posits, "True prayer is exercised in the sphere of the Holy Spirit, motivated and empowered by

Him. The expression praying in the Holy Spirit is also instrumental of means. We pray by means of the Holy Spirit, in dependence on Him."[3]

When we are fully surrendered in God's hands through the working of the Holy Spirit, we learn how to pray according to God's will. The Holy Spirit intercedes on our behalf. And all our needs are satisfied in God's hands, even when He does not give us the exact things we ask of Him. Let us trust God.

CHAPTER 10

Maintaining the First Love

Staying on fire for God requires the rekindling of our first love. Human nature gravitates towards sin. But as Christians, we are called to maintain our love for God as when we first believed. Unfortunately, an enemy works day and night to distract God's people from the truth and confuse their priorities. Satan knows that if the number one priority in one's life is not God, then the spiritual condition will be cold. Scripture tells us that one of the signs of the end is the waning of the love for God. "And because iniquity shall abound, the love of many shall wax cold" (Mathew 24:12 KJV). God gives a strong warning against this condition. To the church of Ephesus, the Lord said,

> I know your works, your labor, your patience, and that you cannot bear those who are evil. And you have tested those who say they are apostles and are not, and have found them liars; and you have persevered and have patience, and have labored for My name's sake and have not become weary. Nevertheless I have this against you, that you have left your first love. Remember therefore from where you have fallen; repent and do the first works, or else I will come to you quickly and remove your lampstand from its place—unless you repent (Revelation 2:2-5)

That was a call to repentance and total surrender to God. Otherwise, the first love would not be rekindled.

The first love "probably included wholehearted love for the truth, and love for one another as brethren and for their fellow men in general. Perhaps the doctrinal controversies stirred up by the false teachers had given rise to a factious spirit . . . To the extent that error had found a lodging place in the church, to the extent was thwarted the activity of the Holy Spirit as a messenger of truth, whose task it is to convert the principles of truth into a living force for the transformation of character."[1]

The problem of losing one's "first love" for God did not end with the church in Ephesus. Throughout the centuries, the church has had to deal with this challenge. The phenomenon of false teachers masquerading as preachers of truth has pulled back the church from carrying out its mission of love. Impostors are all around us. Evil forces are spewing out their spirits on both young and old. Satan is not asleep. He works tirelessly to get people to maintain a lukewarm state in their love for God and His work.

Jesus said that all the law and the prophets are summed up in the two commandments of love. "You shall love the Lord your God with all your heart, with all your soul, and with all your mind. This is *the* first and great commandment. And *the* second *is* like it: You shall love your neighbor as yourself. On these two commandments hang all the Law and the Prophets" (Mathew 22:37-40). Loving God requires our emotional connection (heart), the totality of our being (soul), and the intellectual understanding and affirmation of truth (mind).

The Ephesian Church had not forsaken the Lord. The church did a lot of good religious activities. Doing all that good without love was not working for them. Even though they had not deserted the Lord completely, God was displeased that they had left their "first love." Revelation 2:5 presents both a warning and a solution to the situation: "Remember therefore from where you have fallen; repent and do the first works, or else I will come to you quickly and remove your lampstand from its place—unless you repent."

People often lose their first love for God while still in the church. They drift from loving God with all their hearts to a lukewarm spiritual state. It is unfortunate that people can get so busy in church while their hearts slowly slide away from the truth or from making God their greatest desire.

Through His lovingkindness, God gave the Ephesian Church a chance to repent. He encouraged the church to flashback on their initial love, commitment, and dedication to Him, which they had at the beginning of their spiritual walk with Him. After that, they were to repent. The *King James Bible Dictionary* defines repentance as changing "the mind in consequence of the inconvenience or injury done by past conduct."[2] If the people in the Ephesian Church repented, God would restore them to their first love. But if they refused to repent, God would "remove their lampstand."

If God removes one's lampstand, the person ceases to be a light of the world. That is a sad state to be in. The command to maintain one's first love for God extends to us today. Like the Laodicean Church, God promises to vomit lukewarm people out of His mouth (Revelation 3:16). The church in Laodicea trusted in itself. It felt the need for nothing. It was very secular in its mindset. Yet Jesus described it as blind, naked, and poor. Without God, we reduce ourselves to poverty and public shame. It is dangerous to become complacent in our Christian journey and our relationship with God.

The disciples of Jesus asked Him, "What will be the sign of your coming and of the end of the age?" Among the many signs that Jesus pointed out was that "many false prophets will appear and deceive many people. Because of the increase of wickedness, the love of most will grow cold, but the one who stands firm to the end will be saved" (Mathew 24:11-13). If the times we live in are not the end times, I don't know what is! We are seeing an increase in wickedness right in our own eyes. There is no sense of shame anymore.

Furthermore, we read, "But know this, that in the last days perilous times will come: For men will be lovers of themselves, lovers of money, boasters, proud, blasphemers, disobedient to parents, unthankful, unholy, unloving, unforgiving, slanderers, without self-control, brutal, despisers of good, traitors, headstrong, haughty, lovers of pleasure rather than lovers of God," (2 Timothy 3:1-4). That is humankind's carnal state today. It is the kind that does not allow God to work a change in one's life.

Take a moment and reflect on your experience when you first received Jesus as your Savior. If you notice any difference, what is it? Or remember when you were the most devoted in your faith to God—loving God, loving others, and serving the church. Do you notice any difference? If so, what is it?

Let me share with you my first love experience. I was born into a Christian family. In my high school years, I learned more about God and His Word and surrendered my life to Him. Then, I got baptized into a different church denomination from the one I had attended as a child. As a result, I faced much opposition from my family and others. But from my new faith, I got an experience that I can refer to as my first love experience with God.

Despite the challenges, I was so happy about my new faith. I am very grateful for the first stage of my Christian development when I was just a teenager. God gave me the grace to take me onto another level in my faith. I remember trekking for hours through the woods in Kenya, all by myself, to church and back home. That love experience with God taught me that God is faithful and able to sustain my faith in Him if I let Him.

Today, I remember my love for God and my commitment to Him the first time I got converted. I still love God and others. My whole heart and life belong to Him. I just know that there was something exceptional when I first gave my life entirely to God. And I hope the only difference now is that I am used to my perpetual walk with the Lord.

Also, I pray that I am growing in faith and becoming more like Jesus every day.

God wants us to retain our first love and commitment to Him. Let us take to heart the following warning and reproof:

> Has not Christ been left out of the sermons, and out of the heart? Is there not danger that many are going forward with a profession of the truth, doing missionary work, while the love of Christ has not been woven into the labor? This solemn warning from the True Witness means much; it demands that you shall remember from whence you are fallen, and repent, and do the first works . . . that the church might realize its need of its first ardor of love! When this is wanting, all other excellences are insufficient. The call to repentance is one that cannot be disregarded without peril. A belief in the theory of the truth is not enough.[3]

When we allow the Holy Spirit to work in our hearts, He drives away complacency from our lives. The more we open our hearts to Him, the more He works in us to keep us on fire for God. One of the roles of the Holy Spirit in our lives is to teach us all things. It will take more than a human lifetime on earth to learn "all things." So, learning from the Holy Spirit goes on throughout one's life. The purpose is for us to keep learning and getting transformed into the likeness of our Lord, Jesus Christ.

People often backslide or leave their first love when trials and tribulations come their way. Only God's grace enables God's people to endure tough times in their Christian lives. The *Seventh-day Bible Commentary* says, "it is impossible for man in his own strength to escape from the pit of sin into which he has fallen and to bring forth fruits unto holiness."[4] Without the power of God in us, we can do nothing that will honor God. The spiritual fruit of godliness and holiness that God desires to see in us is only possible through the working of the Holy Spirit.

CHAPTER 11

Faithful Beyond Measure

God has the most powerful resume in the entire universe. In the Bible, we get a glimpse of His constancy. Caleb's life story is one of the many examples in Scripture that demonstrates God's faithfulness to those who trust Him. When the Israelites crossed the Jordan River, and as the people conquered the inhabitants of Canaan, through the power of God, Caleb asked Joshua to let him fight and take a place for himself.

Caleb reminded Joshua how he spied the land way before Moses died. And while other spies expressed fear and doubt about the land, Caleb and Joshua expressed faith that God would give the land to the Israelites. Caleb had the Spirit of God in Him. Thus, through the words of Moses, God had promised that Caleb would one day inherit the land of Canaan. Scripture says:

> Then the children of Judah came to Joshua in Gilgal. And Caleb the son of Jephunneh the Kenizzite said to him: "You know the word which the Lord said to Moses the man of God concerning you and me in Kadesh Barnea. I was forty years old when Moses the servant of the Lord sent me from Kadesh Barnea to spy out the land, and I brought back word to him as it was in my heart. Nevertheless my brethren who went up with me made the heart of the people melt, but I wholly followed the Lord my God. So Moses swore on that day, saying, 'Surely the land where your foot has trodden shall be your inheritance and your children's forever, because you have wholly followed the Lord my God.' And now, behold, the Lord has kept me alive, as He said, these forty-five years, ever since the Lord spoke this word to Moses while Israel wandered in the wilderness; and now, here I am this day, eighty-five years old . . . Now therefore, give me this mountain of which the Lord spoke in that day; for you heard in that day how the Anakim were there, and that the cities were great *and* fortified. It may be that the Lord will be with me, and I shall be able to drive them out as the Lord said." (Joshua 14:6-12)

Caleb's story portrays a man of courage and much faith in God. By this time, Caleb was 85 years old. But since he had the Spirit of God and faith in Him, he asked Joshua to allow him to fight the Anakim, who occupied the mountain of Hebron.

Joshua blessed Caleb. He let him take the land that he desired. Yes, because God is faithful, Caleb got Hebron at 85 years of age. Caleb's story is both encouraging and challenging at the same time. We cannot overemphasize that Caleb trusted God in the deepest sense of the word. As the verses above tell us, all his hope was in God. And as verse 14 tells us, Hebron became Caleb's inheritance because "he wholly followed the Lord God of Israel."

Those who surrender fully to God never get disappointed. God is not like humans, some of whom have no problem betraying trust. But our God is faithful and trustworthy. Because of that, Caleb lived to inherit the land that God had promised him.

Commenting on the book of Joshua, the *Benson Bible Commentary* states that Caleb "was a man of another temper, faithful and courageous, not actuated by that evil spirit of cowardice, unbelief, disobedience, which ruled in his brethren, but by the Spirit of God. 'Hath followed me fully'—Universally and constantly, through difficulties and dangers which made his partners halt."[1] From generation to generation, God has shown His faithfulness and mercy repeatedly. He has the power and faithfulness to fulfill His promises. The book of Psalms says, "They will come and declare His righteousness to a people who will be born, That He has done this" (Ps 22:31).

Let me tell you a short story about my experience with faithfulness while dealing with my father, Peter Kilundo Muthembwa, now deceased. My parents planned to take me to a day high school in Nairobi when I completed Standard 7, the equivalent of Grade 8 in America. My father worked there on a temporary basis. So, the plan was that I would live with him while attending school.

When the day came for me to report to the school, Dad (*Nau* in Kamba language) took me to the school. After all the procedures of admission were completed, he requested that I go back with him so he could train me on crossing roads safely on my way to and from school. The principal granted Nau's request. So, we crossed a few roads toward the bus stop. "Always stop and check both sides of the road before crossing," Nau instructed me.

And after walking for a while, we came to a main road. I approached it consciously and stood on the side to check both sides of the road, as Nau had told me. But instead of Nau stopping beside me, he walked straight into the street. And the next thing I saw was Nau under a big army truck.

Thank God he did not die. But he suffered a broken arm and bruises on his chest. The army men took Nau and me to Kenyatta National Hospital and left us there. After hours that seemed like forever, Nau was treated and released to go home.

When the men who hit Nau took us on the truck to take us to the hospital, I took Nau's arm from his back and put it on his side. It seemed like only the skin was holding it to the rest of the body. Yet, those who attended Nau at the hospital did not put a plaster on the arm or give him painkillers. They wrapped the arm with a bandage and sent us to the estate.

I was the only one with Nau in Nairobi. My mother and siblings were in a rural area about 90 miles away. Roads were less developed than today, and vehicles were extremely few then, especially in rural areas. So, to go from the village to Nairobi was a full day's journey. Hence, it was Nau and me in this near-death sickness.

Later, the hospital put a plaster on Nau's arm, and his health improved after about a month of shock, praying, and crying for his healing. But he still stayed out of work for many months. And since he worked part-time, he had no regular income assistance. Consequently, Nau's accident forced me to drop out of school that year. And when his life seemed out of danger, my concern shifted from his life to my education. The thought of dropping out of school made me cry a lot.

Then Nau made a promise to me. He told me, "Eka kuia. Ngakusomethya ukole kisomo neue." That means, "Do not cry. I will educate you until you say, 'Enough of education.'" Guess what? He did. Nau kept his promise to me. After several months, he recovered and went back to work.

My parents took me to an Adventist boarding school the following year, where I learned more about Jesus and did well in school. And Nau did not stop educating me until I completed the Advanced Level of Education (A' Level) and became a teacher. That was during a time when extremely few parents educated girls beyond high school. Many of them did not go to high school.

Yes, Nau was faithful, but God's faithfulness goes beyond what parents do for their children. Let us trust Him. Let us give all our hearts to Him. Let us seek God and ask for the filling of the Holy Spirit and whatever else we need. By asking for the Holy Spirit, we ask more of Jesus and His power to live Godly lives and to serve Him.

CHAPTER 12

Growing Spiritually

Spiritual Growth entails becoming more and more like Jesus Christ. It means modeling one's life according to the life of Christ. Growing spiritually means exhibiting the fruit of the Spirit as taught in Galatians 5:22-23—"love, joy, peace, forbearance, kindness, goodness, faithfulness, gentleness, and self-control." Manifesting these in one's life takes the working of the Holy Spirit, which goes on for a lifetime.

The Bible also calls this sanctification, that is, continually growing in Christ. When we grow spiritually, we glorify God in our lives. It is not the work of human effort but that of God's grace through the work of the Holy Spirit. Jesus said: "Therefore you shall be perfect, just as your Father in heaven is perfect" (Mathew 5:48). That is the standard that God set for spiritual growth—reaching maturity of Christlike character. This is not referring to achieving a state of sinlessness or perfectionism. According to *Ellicott's Commentary*, "Perfection is not something attained but exists eternally, but we draw near to it and become partakers of the divine nature when we love as He loves."[1]

Even though Christians may never reach the state of perfection in this life, the attitude of a surrendered Christian abhors sin. God should take center stage daily, lead, and guide one's life. Every known sin is confessed and overcome by the grace of God.

The seed of holiness that the Holy Spirit plants in the life of a surrendered Christian keeps growing throughout life. White says, "Every living Christian will advance daily in the divine life. As he advances toward perfection, he experiences a conversion to God every day; and this conversion is not completed until perfection of Christian character is attained and a full preparation for the finishing touch of immortality. God should be the highest object of our thoughts. Meditating upon him, and pleading with him, elevate the soul and quicken the affections."[2] If Christ dwells in the heart, there will be spiritual growth in the life of a Christian. Spiritual weaknesses will be overcome. There will be a deep desire to share the Word of God with others.

Every growth, whether in humans, plants, or animals, is a process. Just like plants require nourishment to grow, so does spiritual growth. I like gardening. And as expected, plants need nutrients, water, sunlight, air, and the right temperature. While different plants may require different ways of care, one thing stands out. All living plants need water. When they go for days without water, they start to wilt. Thus, I constantly water my plants. And just as plants need water, so does every living Christian need the living water daily. What do I mean?

Jesus introduced this living water to a Samaritan woman, saying, "If you knew the gift of God, and who it is who says to you, 'Give Me a drink,' you would have asked Him, and He would have given you living water . . . Whoever drinks of this water will thirst again, but whoever drinks of the water that I shall give him will never thirst. But the water that I shall give him will become in him a fountain of water springing up into everlasting life" (John 4:10, 13, 14). God dwells in the hearts of those who love and obey Him.

As said above, spiritual growth is a lifelong process that keeps people growing in the image of God. In this life, people never reach a spiritual level where they do not need more spiritual growth. Thus, we need constant prayer, reading the Word, and patience. "Spiritual growth is not an event. We don't grow spiritually in just one day. We grow every day, as long as we live."[3] That is why we need daily nourishment.

God's people need to thirst for His presence in their lives. The Holy Spirit stirs that thirst for righteousness. He leads us to the Savior, who is the water of life that satisfies us. The desire for God and the thirst for His Word go together with constant, sincere, daily prayer and obedience. "Only those who are living up to the light they have, will receive greater light. Unless we are daily advancing in the exemplification of the active Christian virtues, we shall not recognize the manifestations of the Holy Spirit as the latter rain. It may be falling on hearts all around us, but we shall not discern or receive it."[4]

We need to be intentional about our spiritual growth. The first step is to admit that we need the Savior, surrender ourselves to Him, feed on the Word of God, and cooperate with Him in every aspect of our lives. We also need spiritual mentoring from mature Christians. Even when we become spiritually mature, we still need constant nourishment of spiritual solid food. "But solid food belongs to those who are of full age, *that is,* those who by reason of use have their senses exercised to discern both good and evil" (Hebrews 5:14). Praying, studying the Word, worshiping (personal and corporate), and sharing the gospel with others keep us firmly connected to the source of wisdom, knowledge, and all needed nutrients for spiritual growth. On the other hand, spiritual malnutrition leads to spiritual death.

As long as we live, there will always be something to learn about God and the process of salvation. God gives us the grace to read the Bible constantly. The power in the Word of God sustains us. The Holy Spirit gives new insight every time we read the Word of God. Without the ministry of the Holy Spirit, there is no spiritual growth.

Every true Christian grows spiritually. Lack of growth indicates a problem. Scripture indicts those who do not allow the Holy Spirit to lead them to spiritual maturity: "For though by this time you ought to be teachers, you need someone to teach you again the first principles of the oracles of God; and you have come to need milk and not solid food" (Hebrews 5:12).

After spending decades in church, church members expect someone to be a mature Christian. The church often calls on people to serve and help teach and encourage "spiritual babies." Unfortunately, there are times a person who is supposed to be a mature Christian turns out to be more immature than many newly converted people.

We saw earlier that the foolish five virgins waited for the groom together with the five wise virgins. Yet, the foolish missed the wedding after waiting for a long time. The foolish ones had lamps just like the wise virgins. Why did the foolish virgins miss the wedding? Because they did not get enough oil for their lamps when they were supposed to do it. As we saw earlier, oil represents the Holy Spirit.

We can always emphasize that there is only spiritual growth with the help of the Holy Spirit. And if one is filled with the Holy Spirit, the fruit will be evident. There will be spiritual growth. The person will continue to grow in holiness. Sin will have no power in that person's life. We read, "But you are not in the flesh but in the Spirit, if indeed the Spirit of God dwells in you. Now if anyone does not have the Spirit of Christ, he is not His" (Romans 8:9). Whoever does not follow the teachings and footsteps of Jesus will not grow spiritually. Will you allow the Holy Spirit to grow you spiritually?

CHAPTER 13

What God Expects of His People

When Jesus comes, He will look for the unique garment of His righteousness. Jesus died to save people from their sins and not to save them in their sins. The Word of God reveals that God expects His people to be holy. The word holy means being set apart or consecrated for a special purpose, which in this case is Godliness. While holiness is our status (those consecrated and set apart), righteousness has to do with our practice (justice, right doing, right attitude, or expected behavior). In the New Testament, holiness refers to those who belong to Christ. Righteousness has to do with reproducing the character of God. Therefore, holiness and righteousness are linked together, even though they are not one and the same thing.

Here, we will be looking at what God expects of His people. God does not just expect righteousness in His people; He teaches them what it means to be righteous and how to receive it. Since nobody is going to heaven while practicing sin, we must know how to become righteous.

God told the Israelites, "For I am the Lord your God. You shall therefore consecrate yourselves, and you shall be holy; for I am holy." (Leviticus 11:44). The Lord did not expect holiness from the Israelites only. He expects the same standard of holiness for us today. We read, "But as He who called you is holy, you also be holy in all your conduct, because it is written, 'Be holy, for I am holy'" (1 Peter 1:15, 16).

The KJV *Bible Dictionary* defines righteousness as "purity of heart and rectitude of life; conformity of heart and life to the divine law."[1] In other words, righteousness refers to moral behavior that conforms to God's law. We see that rectitude is "morally correct behavior or thinking; righteousness."[2] From these definitions and Scripture, God expects His people to be holy in their thoughts, desires, and conduct. He expects them to conform to all teachings in His Word, including the Ten Commandments.

Yes, God knows our thoughts and cares about our deeds and motives behind every act. Oftentimes, we are obsessed with human actions and judge people based on those actions. God, instead, looks deeper into thoughts and motives. Thus, Jesus said a person does not have to commit adultery physically in order to sin. Anyone who looks at a woman lustfully already commits adultery with her in his heart (Matthew 5:28). This is a tall order for human beings in their sinful nature.

Prophet Isaiah wrote: "I will greatly rejoice in the Lord, My soul shall be joyful in my God; For He has clothed me with the garments of salvation, He has covered me with the robe of righteousness, As a bridegroom decks himself with ornaments; And as a bride adorns herself with her jewels. For as the earth brings forth its bud, As the garden causes the things that are sown in it to spring forth, So the Lord God will cause righteousness and praise to spring forth before all the nations" (Isaiah 61:10,11). In God, humans have hope of righteousness and eternal life.

God takes the initiative to seek the lost. He offers salvation and holiness through grace. All He asks is that people cooperate with Him. Yet, throughout generations, humankind has sought righteousness on their terms. They refuse to follow God's guidelines for righteousness. Prophet Isaiah pointed out this same problem in the children of Israel. They worshiped and offered sacrifices to God while their hearts were far from Him. Unfortunately, God called their sacrifices "futile." He told His chosen people that their "incense" was "an abomination" to Him (Isaiah 1:13).

I am glad that God did not stop there. He instructed His people on what to do to be acceptable in His sight. He said: "Wash yourselves, make yourselves clean; Put away the evil of your doings from before My eyes. Cease to do evil, Learn to do good; Seek justice, Rebuke the oppressor; Defend the fatherless, Plead for the widow" (Isaiah 1:16,17).

Righteousness is the abhorrence of sin and any appearance of evil. God's righteousness and salvation have always been by grace, meaning it is what God does in us on the basis of our relationship with Jesus Christ. In Abraham's case, faith was a major factor. He believed in God; as a result, he was termed righteous (Genesis 15:6). Those who accept Jesus as their Savior and Lord repent their sins and turn away from them and are counted justified (forgiven).

God forgives all who repent of their sins. He cleanses them from all unrighteousness and covers them with His righteousness. Total surrender to God and obedience to His revealed will lead to righteousness. "For the Lord *is* righteous, He loves righteousness; His countenance beholds the upright" (Psalm 11:7). Our Savior, "Who Himself bore our sins in His own body on the tree, that we, having died to sins, might live for righteousness—by whose stripes you were healed" (1 Peter 2:24), will see us through. By accepting

Jesus as our Savior and Lord of our lives, we get the grace to die to sin, for there is power in His blood.

Further, we read, "For as by one man's disobedience many were made sinners, so also by one Man's obedience many will be made righteous... so that as sin reigned in death, even so grace might reign through righteousness to eternal life through Jesus Christ our Lord" (Romans 5:19, 21).

The Holy Spirit leads human beings to the Savior and keeps them in the path of righteousness. Jesus promised that the Helper would "convict the world of sin, and of righteousness, and of judgment" (John 16:8). The Holy Spirit speaks to people's hearts and convinces them that they are sinners in need of repentance and yielding to God. The Holy Spirit teaches sinners the truths of God while pointing them to the Lord Jesus Christ.

The Holy Spirit enables sinners to understand that they can be counted righteous if they believe in Jesus. Scripture is clear that people get covered in God's righteousness when they believe in Jesus Christ (Romans 10:4). The indwelling Holy Spirit in a person's heart produces the character of God, which is righteousness.

The important work of the Holy Spirit in moving a person from sin to righteousness was evident in the life of Paul, who gained so much victory in His life. Eventually,

Paul declared, "I have been crucified with Christ; it is no longer I who live, but Christ lives in me; and the life which I now live in the flesh I live by faith in the Son of God, who loved me and gave Himself for me" (Galatians 2:20).

We can only be covered with the righteousness of God if we have the Holy Spirit in our hearts. All the transformation in our lives comes through the Holy Spirit. Total surrender to God makes this possible (1 John 2:29). We can never over-emphasize the need to depend wholly on the Holy Spirit to grow in righteousness.

I grew up on a farm; my parents were farmers. And so, my siblings and I were all trained to be farmers, among other things. In the village, very few people could afford to pay people to work on their farms. So, every family did their own planting, weeding, and harvesting. Sometimes, the work became too much for some people, especially those who did not have many people in their families. Also, those who became sick or had a seriously ill person in their family could not manage to take care of the sick and keep up with the demands of the farm.

But there was a way to get help from one's neighbors. The farm owner invited several people in the community or village to come and help with planting, weeding, or harvesting. Usually, the one getting the help would cook the best food possible to feed those who came to help. Also, whenever people requested help from others, they went to work on the farm together with the helpers. It was unheard of to invite people to one's farm to work while the farm owner remained home. But even though the host worked with the helpers, he or she made sure that there was someone at home to cook for the people so that by the time they were too tired to work, they came to the house to eat the best food the host could afford.

Unlike life on a traditional farm, the Holy Spirit, an invited guest, is the one who works and feeds the host. The Holy Spirit brings the most nutritious and delicious food of all time to share. The Holy Spirit comes into our lives with all blessings and power. He also gives us various gifts with which to serve the Lord. Let us cooperate with Him.

CHAPTER 14

Manifestations of the Holy Spirit

One of the metaphors that identify Christians is that they are the branches. In the Gospel of John, branches must remain attached to the vine in order to bear fruit. "As the branch cannot bear fruit of itself, unless it abides in the vine, neither can you, unless you abide in Me" (John 15: 4). Christ designates Himself as the True Vine. To bear fruit, we must remain in Christ. Christ came to earth to save and teach us how to live and bear fruit to God's glory.

Bearing fruit to God's glory results from allowing the Holy Spirit to dwell in our hearts. The Holy Spirit's presence produces the fruit in us, which enables us to shine as lights to the world. We cannot be the light to the world if we don't practice what we believe. Moreover, if another power is in us, the same will show to other people. If we have Christ in us, we will lead a powerful Christian life.

We read, "He who professes to be in Christ is expected to bring forth fruits appropriate to his profession. These fruits are elsewhere termed 'the fruit of the Spirit' (Gal. 5:22; Eph. 5:9) or 'fruits of righteousness' (Phil. 1:11; cf. Heb. 12), that is, fruits which are righteousness. These fruits are evident in the character and the life. When these 'good fruits' (James 3:17) are absent, it becomes necessary to sever the fruitless branch."[1]

For us to bear fruit to God's glory, we need to remain in a vital relationship with Jesus (John 15). If we abide in Christ, we will bear fruit to God's glory. The world will see God's love, compassion, longsuffering, forgiveness, and joy. Have you ever interacted with someone and felt like you had been with Jesus at the end of the day?

That is how I felt when a certain lady visited my school. The school had recently hired her son, so she visited to see how he was doing. And she needed somewhere to sleep. Students, teachers, and staff lived on campus. So, I accommodated her. A few hours after she came to my dwelling place, I could tell she was a godly woman and a mature Christian. She was on campus for about four days, but I still remember her grace and spiritual maturity twelve years later. By the end of her stay, I felt like I had accommodated Jesus Himself. So, how does the fruit grow in us?

Psalm 1:1-3 tells us how a Godly person bears fruit. We read,

"Blessed is the man
Who walks not in the counsel of the ungodly,
Nor stands in the path of sinners,
Nor sits in the seat of the scornful;
But his delight is in the law of the Lord,
And in His law he meditates day and night.
He shall be like a tree Planted by the rivers of water,
That brings forth its fruit in its season
Whose leaf also shall not wither;
And whatever he does shall prosper."

To meditate on the law of the Lord means one loves the Lord and treasures His Word. Psalm 1 is one of the Bible texts that I recited from childhood. Today, I refer to Psalm 1 in many situations in life. I love many things about this text. First, the righteous person gets the power to overcome evil. That is what God does in the lives of those who abide in Him. Second, I love the promise that the blessed person seeks God and His righteousness. I see love, joy, peace, satisfaction, contentment, and every good thing in that sentence alone—no wonder the person is blessed.

As I said before, a plant goes through a process for it to bear fruit. It starts from the seed that is planted. When it germinates, it grows by feeding on nutrients from the soil; it needs water, sunlight, and air. Eventually, the plant bears fruit. We also know that many fruit trees bear fruit when they are pruned. Similarly, Christians must undergo the same process. Thus, endurance, faith, and trust in God are needed to allow the pruning to take place.

Earlier, we saw that fruit-bearing means attaining and portraying the character of God in one's life. Jesus will look for His character in those He will take with Him to heaven. Thus, it is crucial to develop the character of God in each one of us. White says,

> The Saviour . . . points out the sign of discipleship: 'Herein is my Father glorified, that ye bear much fruit; so shall ye be my disciples.' By faith, we are to lay hold on a living God and maintain an experience that shall breathe love, tenderness, kindness, compassion, and affection. These traits of character are the fruit that the Lord Jesus desires us to produce and to present before the world as a witness that we have a Saviour who can uplift and who can satisfy . . . What we need is the presence of Jesus Christ. We want His truth shining in our hearts, pervading all our life actions. This will determine whether or not we are branches of the True Vine.[2]

When we emulate Jesus, we bear the fruit of righteousness. Christ did not live for Himself. He honored His Father and endured suffering for our benefit. As His followers, we are called to love God and other people. God wants us to serve the church, help others grow spiritually, pray with and for others, and encourage them to trust in God.

CHAPTER 15

Pointing Others to the Savior

Saying there is a great need for laborers in God's vineyard is an understatement. In this chapter, God's vineyard refers to God's work. Jesus said to His disciples, "The harvest truly is great, but the laborers are few; therefore pray the Lord of the harvest to send out laborers into His harvest" (Luke 10:2). Jesus said these words to the seventy disciples whom He sent out to preach the kingdom of God. These words are as valid today as when the Lord first spoke to the disciples. Why? Because there are still many who need to hear the good news and accept the Savior.

Right in our families, neighborhoods, villages, towns, and big cities, people need to know the love of God for them. There is a need to teach others about the Savior who gives peace and joy to every troubled heart. It is one thing to hear about God. It is another to realize the need to repent and turn away from sins. God provides the power to overcome any obstacle.

The disciples experienced it. Luke 10:17 tells us, "Then the seventy returned with joy, saying, "Lord, even the demons are subject to us in Your name." What can't we achieve for God under the leadership of the Holy Spirit? Jesus told the disciples to rejoice not because they were in control of demons but because their names were in the Book of Life (Luke 10:20). Eternal life is the highest goal and reward in witnessing and all our service to God.

The Lord wants His followers to witness and point others to Him. The Holy Spirit gives various spiritual gifts to God's people to use in His service. Witnessing for God is only possible when we use our Holy Spirit-given gifts.

In 2022, I witnessed a situation in my church that taught me that there is a great need for more prayer for the Holy Spirit to work in God's people. For about seven months, our church was without a senior pastor. The one we had accepted a call elsewhere after serving in our church for about twelve years. The church had three pastors for years. But when the senior pastor transferred, we remained with two in a church that was said to require four pastors. As a church and individuals, we prayed for a senior pastor who could lead a big multicultural church in America. The conference, working with the church, set up a search committee. We searched for months without success. As a church board member, I was much involved in this process. In the end, I learned that there is a great need for surrendered, committed, mature laborers in God's vineyard. Even though we have many such servants of God, more are needed.

The question still to be answered, though, is why the search committee failed to find a qualified senior pastor among various pastors throughout the country. Perhaps, in addition to all the answers that can be given here, it was God's way of telling us that what mattered was not the number of pastors we had to do the work but that the work was in the hands of the laity. Whatever the case, in God's vineyard, laborers are needed at all levels.

Many times, God commissioned people to perform various duties for Him. And when He did, He equipped them with His Spirit, who enabled them to do the work. For example, when the Lord appointed Aaron to serve Him as a priest, He instructed Moses to ensure that holy garments were made for Aaron as the priest. And who was to make the holy garments? God said to Moses, "So you shall speak to all who are gifted artisans, whom I have filled with the spirit of wisdom, that they may make Aaron's garments, to consecrate him, that he may minister to Me as priest" (Exodus 28:3).

Furthermore, we see what God did before He sent Ezekiel to the people of Israel. "And He said to me, 'Son of man, stand on your feet, and I will speak to you. Then the Spirit entered me when He spoke to me, and set me on my feet; and I heard Him who spoke to me. And He said to me: 'Son of man, I am sending you to the children of Israel, to a rebellious nation that has rebelled against Me; they and their fathers have transgressed against Me to this very day'" (Ezekiel 2:1-3). When God called Ezekiel to serve Him as a prophet, He gave him the Holy Spirit.

When Moses got overwhelmed by leadership responsibilities, God instructed him to get seventy leaders of Israel. The seventy were to help Moses with leadership duties. But before they started performing the work, God took some portion of the Holy Spirit in Moses and gave it to the seventy men. Immediately the Holy Spirit rested on them, they prophesied (Numbers 11:16-25).

Jesus Christ Himself was baptized with both water and the Holy Spirit before He started His ministry (Mathew 3:16). Thus, He was empowered to face the temptations of Satan and to establish His ministry of saving the lost. Christ's ministry was so strong that more than two thousand years later, it continues. If Christ received the Holy Spirit before

He began His ministry, it means that before we can start any work for God, we should pray for the daily filling of the Holy Spirit for power and guidance.

God gave His Holy Spirit to the people He called to serve. Scripture tells us, "Be filled with the Spirit" (Ephesians 5:18). We need to be filled continually. God has given work to every single Christian. He wants us to teach others the good news, which will not happen without the Holy Spirit's teaching, guidance, and empowerment.

White tells us, "For the daily baptism of the Spirit, every worker should offer his petition to God. Companies of Christian workers should gather to ask for special help, for heavenly wisdom, that they may know how to plan and execute wisely. Especially should they pray that God will baptize His chosen ambassadors in mission fields with a rich measure of His Spirit."[1]

The Bible records many different experiences of people, some who totally surrendered to God, others who were hypocrites, and others who were outright evil workers. These help us to learn and know what to expect depending on our response to God's grace. For example, we read about Paul's surrender to God and dedication to His work. As a result, Scripture presents Paul with so much power of the Spirit that his "handkerchiefs or aprons were brought from his body to the sick, and the diseases left them and the evil spirits went out of them" (Acts 19:11).

We also see examples of people who had a financial motive for doing God's work. For example, some Jewish exorcists decided to call on the name of Jesus over someone who was possessed by evil spirits. Then something interesting happened. The evil spirits mocked the exorcists. A Swahili-speaking person would say, *Shetani anamadharau sana,* meaning that Satan is highly contemptuous. Look at what transpired in the following verses. "'We exorcise you by the Jesus whom Paul preaches." Also there were seven sons of Sceva, a Jewish chief priest, who did so. And the evil spirit answered and said, "Jesus I know, and Paul I know; but who are you?" Then the man in whom the evil spirit was leaped on them, overpowered them, and prevailed against them, so that they fled out of that house naked and wounded" (Acts 19:13-16). The exorcists said, "We exorcise you by the Jesus whom Paul preaches."

These men were playing games with the name of Jesus. They had no relationship with Jesus. They did not have Christ in them. They did not have the Holy Spirit in them. So, the evil spirits fought them and overpowered them. Evil spirits in one man fought several men until they "fled the house naked and wounded." This defeat did not end with the exorcists we see in Acts 19. Professing Christians suffer all sorts of unnecessary defeat against Satan and his agents.

Christians are to have their spiritual power refilled daily. Yes, they need spiritual retooling daily. When God's people relax in praying or allow distractions from worldly pursuits, they become spiritually weak. Worse still, when people go to church without a living relationship with the Savior, they will undoubtedly suffer defeat against the enemy. It was not without a good reason that Jesus told His disciples to wait until they received the Holy Spirit before they went out to spread the kingdom of God. The disciples could only destroy the kingdom of Satan with divine power. Without God's presence, we cannot succeed in God's work.

The Holy Spirit does not only win spiritual battles for God's people in mission work but also guides every step of the way. Acts 16:6 tells us that Paul and Timothy went through Phrygia and the region of Galatia, intending to preach the gospel in Asia. But the Holy Spirit forbade them. At the time, the Holy Spirit had a different plan for them. Every Christ's follower needs this kind of guidance every step of the way. Whether in our personal lives or in ministry, we need the Holy Spirit to lead us.

Christ instructed His disciples to wait in prayer for needed power in ministry. The disciples received the blessing after the Pentecost baptism. They were empowered for success. If the disciples who had been with Jesus for more than three years needed to wait for empowerment by the Holy Spirit before they went to the world to spread the gospel, we need that, too.

But are we praying for the filling of the Holy Spirit? Morris L. Venden says, "The tragedy of Laodicea is that so many have experienced only the first work of the Holy Spirit," which is 'conviction of sin and conversion.' "They know they are sinners. They have been convicted of judgment to come. They may have even, at one time, surrendered themselves to God and experienced the new birth. But they stopped right there and have never continued seeking and praying and desiring the deeper spiritual life."[2]

In *The Desire of Ages*, we read, "In order to serve Him [God] aright, we must be born of the divine Spirit. This will purify the heart and renew the mind, giving us a new capacity for knowing and loving God."[3] That is what we need as Christians.

CHAPTER 16

Completing the Journey Well

Every genuine Christian desires to complete the journey to heaven well. Apostle Paul gives us the true meaning of completing the journey well. Towards the end of his life, he wrote: "I have fought the good fight, I have finished the race, I have kept the faith. Finally, there is laid up for me the crown of righteousness, which the Lord, the righteous Judge, will give to me on that day, and not to me only but also to all who have loved His appearing" (2 Timothy 4:7, 8). Paul was confident that he had done God's will in the deepest sense possible. Even though he still had more work to spread the gospel, he had no regrets about how he had served and the much he had already accomplished. He knew that others would carry on with the work from where he would stop. That is what it means to work for God. You do your part faithfully and realize that you are not alone but in partnership with others.

The message in this last chapter is well summarized in the following verses: "Therefore we also, since we are surrounded by so great a cloud of witnesses, let us lay aside every weight, and the sin which so easily ensnares us, and let us run with endurance the race that is set before us, looking unto Jesus, the author and finisher of our faith, who for the joy that was set before Him endured the cross, despising the shame, and has sat down at the right hand of the throne of God" (Hebrews 12:1, 2). What do these verses mean?

The *Seventh-day Adventist Bible Commentary* analyzes the verses above very well. It says,

> The writer leaves it to each reader to discover what may be hampering his progress as a Christian runner . . . Every man has some besetting sin, some tendency to evil that seeks to impede him as he runs the race. When he gains the victory over that particular evil propensity, another takes its place and presses for the mastery. Thus the pathway of salvation is beset by one battle after another. But it is every Christian's privilege to achieve victory each step of the way . . . Because the Christian race is a lifelong experience, it calls for patience and perseverance—perseverance in the face

of successive difficulties and disappointments and patience to await the reward at the end of the course.[1]

If Christian life were easy, there would be no need for such words as endurance and perseverance in the Bible. Nobody endures an easy life. An easy life is enjoyed, not endured. So, God does not call us to an easy life. It was not easy for the prophets, our Savior, the disciples of Jesus, and the early Christians like Stephen. Yet, they lived godly lives and served God by faith.

The same grace that empowered Peter, Paul, and others to live godly lives and successfully serve the Lord in the past is available to us today. Jesus died to avail that grace to us and make peace with God for us. Paul says, "For through Him we both have access by one Spirit to the Father" (Ephesians 2:18). Yes, through Jesus, we have access to God, and the Holy Spirit ensures that we have our connection and relationship with Jesus for our salvation. The unity of God the Father, the Son, and the Holy Spirit is inevitable for our salvation.

On earth, the Holy Spirit helps us run our race well, right to the finish line. In heaven, Jesus, the "author and finisher of our faith" (Hebrews 12:2), represents us before the Father to ensure our ultimate salvation. As Hebrews 4:14-16 says, Jesus understands what we are going through. For our sake,

He endured every difficulty, trial, shame, and pain, including the cross.

Moreover, as we work diligently to complete the journey well, God wants us to help others. He gives us the grace to encourage others to give their lives to the Savior. Satan does not let that happen without interference. The devil wants everyone to be lost. And he is never in shortage of ways of distracting people from God to the vanities of this life. The devil promotes his evil propaganda through the Internet, social media, television, radio, and print media channels. Thus, evil is being relativized and normalized.

Completing our journey on earth well requires a strong connection between us and the Savior, Jesus Christ. With all the distractions and confusion in the world, total focus on God takes the grace of God. Unless we love Jesus, we will get distracted by the voices of evil that surround us on every side. When we surrender fully to God, He gives us victory and guides us home. His Word and Spirit will direct our path.

Scripture reveals to us all we need to know to prepare for our Lord's coming. We do well to study the Word of God, accept its teachings, and obey its commands. Satan knows the message in the Bible very well, but his knowledge does not transform him. He remains evil. Head knowledge of Scripture without total surrender to God, which includes obedience and the filling of the Holy Spirit, is nothing.

Again, the story of the ten virgins who waited for the bridegroom demonstrates our present situation in getting ready for the second coming of Jesus (Mathew 25:1-13). As we read in the parable, the five virgins were wise because they had enough oil in their lamps to last the whole time. The foolish five virgins, instead, did not have enough. Weddings during those days were known for potential delays. The foolish virgins should have anticipated that possibility and brought extra supplies of oil. In other words, they lacked adequate preparedness.

Many times in the Bible, the Holy Spirit is referred to as the spirit of wisdom (James 1:5). That is what the five foolish virgins lacked—the Holy Spirit, the spirit of wisdom to remain alert and expectant. The *Seventh-day Bible Commentary* explains:

> In this parable, the ten young women represent all of those who profess the pure faith of Jesus. They believe in the soon coming of Jesus . . . The lamps represent the Word of God . . . The five foolish maidens are not hypocrites. They are 'foolish' in that they had not yielded themselves to the working of the Holy Spirit . . . The wise virgins of the parable represent those Christians who understand, appreciate, and avail themselves of the ministry of the Holy Spirit. 'Wise' indeed are Christians today who

> welcome the Holy Spirit into their lives and cooperate with Him in His appointed task.[2]

Let us allow the Holy Spirit to lead us in our preparation for heaven. Will you?

Conclusion

In conclusion, those who want to be ready for heaven when Jesus comes must undergo justification (forgiveness) and sanctification (continual Christian growth). They accept Jesus as their Savior and allow spiritual growth to continue in their lives. The Holy Spirit knocks at the heart of a sinner, entreating the sinner to accept Jesus Christ as a Savior. He convicts of sin and leads the sinner toward repentance. Once the sinner accepts Jesus as Savior, the Holy Spirit continues teaching and empowering the person to cooperate with God in all areas of one's life.

The converted sinner accepts water baptism. During that process, the Holy Spirit confirms the new member by sealing the person for redemption. We read, "And do not grieve the Holy Spirit of God, by whom you were sealed for the day of redemption" (Ephesians 4:30). This member is now God's possession throughout life until the day of redemption when

Jesus comes. Jesus and the Holy Spirit remain active agents throughout one's life.

White tells us, "It was by the confession and forsaking of sin, by earnest prayer and consecration of themselves to God, that the early disciples prepared for the outpouring of the Holy Spirit on the Day of Pentecost. The same work, only in greater degree, must be done now."[3]

As we wait for the second coming of our Lord, let us heed the Word of God: "Therefore do not let sin reign in your mortal body, that you should obey it in its lusts. And do not present your members *as* instruments of unrighteousness to sin, but present yourselves to God as being alive from the dead, and your members *as* instruments of righteousness to God" (Romans 6: 11-13).

God saves. He sustains His own in righteousness and will lead them to heaven. But we need to cooperate with Him. For this to happen, there is a great need for the filling of the Holy Spirit, who produces the character of God in those who let Him. The image of God must be restored in those who want to dwell with the Savior in the new Jerusalem.

The Holy Spirit was given to prepare people for the kingdom. "The work started in the power of the Holy Spirit, as the early rain. And the work will finish in the Holy Spirit in the latter rain. The latter rain will be more abundant than the early rain. But only those who devote their lives to prayer will receive the Holy Spirit to help finish the mission."[4]

We cannot overemphasize the fact that for us to be ready to go to heaven, we need to surrender ourselves fully to God, allow for the filling of the Holy Spirit, and obey the Word of God. "By this we know that we abide in Him, and He in us, because He has given us of His Spirit" (1 John 4:13). Let us choose life.

ENDNOTES

Chapter 1 Unseen Danger

1. Seventh-day Adventist Bible Commentary, Exodus (Hagerstown, Md: Review and Herald Publishing Association, 1980), p. 585.

2. Ellen G. White., *The Desire of Ages*, 123, accessed July 11, 2023.https://whiteestate.org/devotional/flb/01_17/.

3. Ellen G. White. *The Great Controversy*, 517, accessed July 11, 2023.https://www.ellenwhite.info/books/ellen-g-white-book-great-controversy-gc-31.htm.

4. Seventh-day Bible Commentary, 1 Peter (Hagerstown, Md: Review and Herald Publishing Association, 1980), p. 587.

5. Ellen G. White. *The Acts of The Apostles*, 59-50, accessed July 11, 2023.https://m.egwwritings.org/en/book/87.463.

6. Ellen G. White. *In Heavenly Places*, 266, accessed July 2023.https://m.egwwritings.org/en/book/38.1949#1954.

Chapter 2 Receiving the Best Gifts

1. Morris L. Venden, *Your Friend The Holy Spiri*t (Boise, ID: Pacific Press Publishing Association, 1986), p. 8.

2. LeRoy E. Froom, *The Coming of the Comforter* (Washington, DC: Review and Herald Publishing Association, 1949), p. 43.
3. Ellen G. White, *The Desire of Ages*, 669, accessed October 10, 2022. https://whiteestate.org/devotional/flb/02_19/.
4. Ellen G. White, *The Acts of the Apostles*, 50, accessed May 27, 2021. https://www.ellenwhite.info/books/ellen-g-white-book-acts-of-the-apostles-aa-05.htm.

Chapter 3 The Overlooked Need

1. LeRoy E. Froom, *The Coming of the Comforter* (Washington, DC: Review and Herald Publishing Association, DC: 1949), p. 131.
2. Ibid., p. 143
3. Ellen G. White. *The Desire of Ages*, 805, accessed October 10, 2022. https://whiteestate.org/devotional/flb/02_20/.
4. Ellen G. White. *The Acts of the Apostles*, 51, accessed 10/10/2022, https://www.ellenwhite.info/books/ellen-g-white-book-acts-of-the-apostles-aa-05.htm.

Chapter 4 Receiving the Holy Spirit

1. Ellen G. White, *Testimonies for the Church*, 8:19, accessed November 10, 2022. https://m.egwwritings.org/en/book/13.1753.

2. LeRoy E. Froom, *The Coming of the Comforter* (Washington, DC: Review and Herald Publishing Association, 1949), p. 142.
3. Ellen G. White, *The Acts of the Apostles*, 37, accessed November 10, 2022. https://m.egwwritings.org/en/book/127.128.
4. Pavel Goia & Kelly Mowrer, *In The Spirit and Power: God's Presence and Answers to Prayer in Pavel Goia's journey*, (Sefeliz USA, 2022), 80.
5. Ellen G. White. *Testimonies to Ministers and Gospel Workers*, 169.2, accessed May 22, 2023, https://m.egwwritings.org/en/book/123.961.
6. LeRoy E. Froom. The Coming of the Comforter, (Review and Herald Publishing Association, DC: Washington, 1949), 142.

Chapter 5 Seeking God Diligently

1. *Seventh-day Adventist Bible Commentary*, John, (Hagerstown, Md: Review and Herald Publishing Association, 1980), p. 940.
2. Ellen G. White, *Counsels to Parents, Teachers, and Students*, 460.1, accessed April 1, 2023.https://m.egwwritings.org/en/book/23.2264#2265.
3. Seventh-day Adventist Bible Commentary, on Mathew (Hagerstown, Md: Review and Herald Publishing Association, 1980), p. 356.

Chapter 6 The Audacity to Ask

1. E. M. Bounds, *E. M. Bounds on Prayer* (New Kensington, PA: Whitaker House 1997), p. 143.

2. Ellen G. White. *Prayer*, 8.1, accessed June 3, 2023.https://m.egwwritings.org/en/book/87.20#26.

Chapter 7 The Role of Faith in Asking

1. *Seventh-day Adventist Bible Commentary*, Genesis (Hagerstown, Md: Review and Herald Publishing Association, 1978), p. 482.

2. Mission Venture Ministries, https://missionventureministries.wordpress.com/2018/12/27/what-is-the-fundamental-nature-of-faith-hebrews-111/.

Chapter 8 Claiming God's Promises

1. LeRoy E. Froom, *The Coming of the Comforter* (Washington, DC: Review and Herald Publishing Association, 1949), p. 187.

Chapter 9 Allowing God to Transform Your Desires

1. King James Version Bible Dictionary, "Desire," accessed July 14, 2023. https://av1611.com/kjbp/kjv-dictionary/desirable.html.

2. Ellen G. White, *Testimonies for the Church*, 5:200.4, accessed June 14, 2023.https://m.egwwritings.org/en/book/113.1021#1025.

3. CS. Lewis, *Prayer,* accessed June 14, 2023. https://www.cslewisinstitute.org/resources/praying-in-the-spirit/.

Chapter 10 Maintaining the First Love

1. *Seventh-day Bible Commentary,* Revelation (Hagerstown, Md: Review and Herald Publishing Association, 1978), p. 744.

2. *The King James Bible Dictionary,* "repent," accessed June 12, 2023.https://kingjamesbibledictionary.com/Dictionary/repent.

3. Ellen G. White, *Selected Messages,* Book 1 (Review and Heralds, February 3, 1891), accessed June 12, 2023.

4. *Seventh-day Adventist Bible Commentary,* John (Hagerstown, Md: Review and Herald Publishing Association, 1978), p. 744.

Chapter 11 Faithful Beyond Measure

1. *The Benson Bible Commentary,* Joshua, accessed October 26, 2022.https://biblehub.com/commentaries/numbers/14-24.htm.

Chapter 12 Growing Spiritually

1. Ellicott's Commentary on Matthew 5:48, accessed July 3, 2023.https://biblehub.com/commentaries/matthew/5-48.htm.

2. Ellen G. White, *The Review and Herald August 17*, 1886, para. 3, accessed July 25, 2022. https://m.egwwritings.org/en/book/821.7508#7514.

3. Pavel Goia & Kelly Mowrer, *In The Spirit and Power: God's Presence and Answers to Prayer in Pavel Goia's Journey*, (Sefeliz USA, 2022), p. 56.

4. LeRoy E. Froom, *The Coming of the Comforter* (Washington, DC: Review and Herald Publishing Association, 1949), p. 133.

Chapter 13 God's Expectation of His People

1. *KJV Bible Dictionary,* the definition of righteousness, accessed August 9, 2022.https://av1611.com/kjbp/kjv-dictionary/righteous.html.

2. *Google.com* definition of rectitude, accessed August 9, 2022. https://www.google.com/search?client=firefox-b-1-d&q=rectitude+definition.

Chapter 14 Bearing God's Fruit

1. Seventh-day Adventist Bible Commentary, John (Hagerstown, MD: Review and Heralds Publishing Association, 1978), p. 1042.

2. Ellen G. White, *Fruit-Bearing Branches*, accessed May 31 2022. https://whiteestate.org/devotional/ohc/05_18/.

Chapter 15 Pointing Others to the Savior

1. Ellen G. White, *The Acts of the Apostles*, 50,51, accessed August 8, 2022.https://m.egwwritings.org/en/book/13.1740#1747.
2. Morris L. Venden, *Your Friend, The Holy Spirit* (Boise, ID: Pacific Press Publishing Association, 1986), p. 19.
3. Ellen G. White, *The Desire of Ages*, 189, accessed July 25, 2022.https://m.egwwritings.org/en/book/130.815.

Chapter 16 Completing the Journey Well

1. *Seventh-day Adventist Bible Commentary,* Genesis (Hagerstown, Md: Review and Herald Publishing Association, 1978), p. 482.
2. *Seventh-day Bible Commentary,* Matthew (Hagerstown, Md: Review and Herald Publishing Association, 1978), p. 508.
3. Ellen G. White, *Prayer*, accessed September 3, 2023. https://m.egwwritings.org/en/book/87.610, accessed September 3, 2023.
4. Pavel Goia & Kelly Mowrer, *In The Spirit and Power: God's Presence and Answers to Prayer in Pavel Goia's Journey* (Sefeliz USA, 2022), p. 148.

www.ingramcontent.com/pod-product-compliance
Lightning Source LLC
LaVergne TN
LVHW090613110826
845146LV00001B/366

* 9 7 9 8 9 8 5 7 2 0 5 2 5 *